CONSIDER ENGLAND

CONSIDER
ENGLAND

LINDA PROUD ~ VALERIE PETTS

SHEPHEARD-WALWYN

© text Linda Proud 1994

© watercolours Valerie Petts 1994

First published in 1994 by

Shepheard-Walwyn (Publishers) Ltd

Suite 34, 26 Charing Cross Road

London WC2H 0DH

ISBN 0 85683 145 X

Printed and bound in Great Britain by

The Sherwood Press, Nottingham

CONTENTS

ACKNOWLEDGEMENTS   6

PREFACE   7

THE ENGLAND WE SEE   12

THE LAW IS ABOVE YOU   50

ENGLISH – THE NATION'S TREASURE   76

THE OPEN-AIR CHURCH   106

AFTERWORD   140

BIBLIOGRAPHY   141

INDEX   142

ACKNOWLEDGEMENTS

It has to be said that those most responsible for this book, those 'without whom it would not have been possible', live no more in the mortal realms but are those ancestors who have displayed sagacity, who have loved their nation, who have argued, persuaded, and pushed England towards ideals not of this world. Departed spirits they be, but their ideals were eternal and we thank them for them. We thank also those amongst the living who put truth above popularity, the nation above the individual, and have the courage to speak out as necessary, one of the best and bravest of them all being His Royal Highness, the Prince of Wales. Our families and friends have sustained us with wonderful encouragement. Specifically we thank the following for their generous gifts of time and advice, noting with delight as we do that some of them are English not by birth but by choice: Leslie Blake, Peter Bonnici, Paul Douglas, Claire Foster, Dr Alice Greene, Nicholas Hardyman, David Hipshon, Jenny Luigs, Alan Martin, Ian Mason, Georgina Melville, Chris Murray, Dorine van Oyen, Dr Katherine Watson, Anthony Werner and Henri Schoup.

The following institutions and individuals kindly granted us permission to paint: R.T.G. Chester-Master, cover and p.25; His Royal Highness, the Prince of Wales and his staff at Highgrove, pp.42-3; All Souls College, Oxford, p.58; The Royal Collection, St. James's Palace, p.67; The Curators of the Bodleian Library, Oxford, p.71; The Ditchley Park Foundation, pp.88-9; Oxford University Press, p.100. The following authors and publishers have kindly given us permission to quote: The Hogarth Press for *Cider with Rosie* by Laurie Lee; Christopher Fry and the School of Humanities, King's College, London for *One Thing More or Caedmon Constructed* by Christopher Fry; Sweet and Maxwell Ltd. for *Freedom Under the Law* by Sir Alfred Denning and *Trial by Jury* by Sir Patrick Devlin; The Longman Group UK Ltd. for *Hulsean Lectures, 1926* by Dean Inge. We have endeavoured to contact all the copyright owners and any queries arising should be addressed to the publisher. Further acknowledgements will, if necessary, be included in the next edition.

PREFACE

It is often the case with the English that the more something is treasured, the less it is spoken of. Topics such as truth, peace, justice and beauty are unlikely to arise in everyday conversation, unlikely indeed to arise in everyday thinking. And yet if we would only stop and consider we might see that our lives are being informed by values such as these. They determine the way we conduct ourselves both individually and socially, in standards of personal conduct and the standards the nation requires of its institutions.

Throughout our long history there have been occasions when men have been driven to speak out for these values. Indeed, the very language itself is formed for such speech. The gain for the nation is incalculable: through religious tolerance, for instance, England has gained peace, and through the fine system of law, freedom of the individual. Just as virtues and vices can be read on a man's face, so what a nation values is visible in its landscape. With the overriding sense of the English landscape being one of beauty, it stands to reason that the English nature is perhaps better than most of the English suppose it to be.

The virtue which underlies the English character is what makes England one of the richest nations on earth, and it is this fundamental decency which other nations aspire to when they speak of their desire for 'democracy'. Virtue has not, however, grown from democracy; rather is the opposite true. Parliamentary democracy grew out of virtue, out of a love of freedom. It is the rose in the English garden, created by the hard work of many generations of gardeners.

The landscape is the past. It is the result of all that has gone before: Anglo-Saxon agrarian life, Alfred the Great's new towns, medieval monasteries, yeoman farming, estate management, industrial revolution, suburban growth – all these have formed and are still forming the England which we see.

This book is the product of a search for England's meaning, a search which has taken place in two realms: in touring the island and seeing the landscape, and in reading the histories and literature. Which is to say that the search has been conducted in the dimensions of time and space. As with a maze, one may enter by several gates and the ones chosen here have been law, language and religion. The guides leading the way have been those qualities which the English particularly cherish. Of course there is no quality which is exclusive to the English. Other nations may cherish the same qualities, or may prefer others. Three qualities which, occur often in the words of English writers are truth, freedom and love of wisdom. Each of these underlies a major institution: truth behind language, freedom behind law, wisdom behind religion. To follow the analogy of the maze, each of these is a path from a gate to the centre. Most mazes have a pattern, the pattern of a spiral, or a French parterre, or perhaps of a quincunx knot. As in any formal pattern, elements repeat, so it comes as no surprise to find, for instance, that principles of English law echo in English grammar. Indeed, the closer we get to the centre, the more easy it is to forget which realm it is that we are occupying.

It was Plato who first conceived of 'quality' as a defining essence, the -*ness* of something; defining, that is, in the way that we now understand following the discoveries in the realms of genetics. As with the catness of a cat, for example, the Englishness of the English rests on inbuilt codes. The Spanish poet, Federico Garcia Lorca, once heard an Andalusian mother singing a lullaby to her baby and, in that moment, he realized that *all* Spanish lullabies are profoundly sad, that melancholy is sung into Spanish children by their mothers. The encoding of a nation, the passing on not only of behaviour but of mood from one generation to another, occurs by sound, by speech.

For the English, there may be some muddle with Britishness, and certainly there are many qualities shared with the Scots, Welsh and Irish. In this book, however, we are considering England. Once we get to the heart of Englishness and those defining qualities, once we have reduced the study to its essence, we will come to the code, as it were, not only of the English nation but of the many nations of the English-speaking peoples, in particular North America, Canada, Australia and New Zealand. Unlike some nations, we have no tests of citizenship in England. We can fairly say that all who speak English and live under English law may consider themselves to be English, if they so choose.

Perhaps one of the most surprising discoveries during the research for this work was the strong thread of platonism to be found in many English institutions. This is not accidental. The Anglo-Saxons had contact with the Scythians in the fifth century, who in turn were in contact with the Greeks. The platonic influence of John Crysostom and John Cassian came to Britain via the Irish monks. In the Middle Ages the many translations of *The Consolation of Philosophy* by Boethius injected a strong platonic strain into English religiosity. Since the fifteenth century, when in Italy the corpus of platonic works was translated into Latin, the contact between English thinkers and platonic thought has been direct. Since then there has been a basic division in philosophy, between those who believe in life as the organic unity of the Creator, and those who believe in man and his fate as being the consequence of chaos and accident. The first view tends towards optimism, the second towards pessimism. According to the principles of England's greatest institutions, however, it is the first view that is the true one. This is the hidden platonism of the nation. It is as if quietly, across the centuries, England has taken up the philosophic torch lit in Athens in the fifth century BC, the torch which shines upon such ideals as the freedom of the individual, religious tolerance and just government.

The nature which forms the people of England is the same nature which forms the landscape. That nature is not all pretty: this is no longer the land of little villages, of gentlemen and honest labourers. We retain all these things, but we have added to them. Great conurbations linked by motorways, squalid inner cities and souless suburbs blot the landscape, just as certain reprehensible qualities mar the English character. These things are not celebrated in these pages. Fault-finding is easy whereas self-esteem requires inspiration and positive nurture. To love another, it has been said, one needs first to love oneself. What is true for the individual is true for the nation. England is of no use to Europe or the rest of the world if it is disabled and disfigured by self-criticism.

With the discovery of each great ideal comes the painful awareness of its contrary. As when the eye has rested on one colour it begins to see its complimentary colour, so even as one talks of honesty, integrity and justice in English institutions, instances of their opposites appear in the newspapers. The fact is that it is exceptional events that reach the papers. For each miscarriage of justice there are a thousand occasions when a magistrate or a judge gives the right verdict and a reasonable sentence. For every corrupt policeman there are a thousand doing their proper duty. For each instance of fraud there are a thousand honest business transactions. Today in England we are unable to be complacent or to take for granted any longer those things which we presume to be our natural right. If we do not begin to recognize what good there is in the nation, and applaud it, we stand in danger of losing it.

One of the things that has become obvious during research is that, from the beginning, the story of England has been one of change rather than stasis. Contrary to popular opinion, our institutions are not fossilized but are the living products of centuries of reform. Similarly the language is a living thing and persists in conforming to natural law rather than to academic regulation. As we approach the millenium, we should not fear change, but it would behove us to base further reforms on sound principle rather than on the will of demagogues such as those in the media who seek not the truth but the story.

English literature abounds with the words and wisdom of those who have valued truth. Included here are those jewels that have been found, in the profound hope that they will encourage poets and writers, statesmen and politicians, both present and to come, to speak the truth when the circumstance demands it. Whatever the future holds for the world, the voice of England, which has spoken so often on behalf of all mankind, must not be stilled.

Though the English have never been satisfied with the way things are, they do not urge change so much as resist it. One of the things most stubbornly resisted over the ages is unwonted foreign influence, particularly in the form of government or ideology. The English are perfectly happy to adopt Italian and French fashions in dress, gardening and cookery, but Italian and French attempts to impose deeper values on the English (in the form, for example, of the Roman Church or the Norman overlordship) did not meet with any enduring success. England always reverts to being itself again in time. It does so by means of the language. In the history of the language we see the powerful process of assimilation in action. As the language has taken in a multitude of foreign words and made them conform to English grammar, so the English have taken in a multitude of things foreign, and then submitted them to the process of anglicization.

The formation of the nation has arisen from many factors, but the greatest of these is speech. Our institutions rest entirely on speech. The government, the law, the universities, could all exist without the buildings with which they are associated, but they could not exist without speech. Oxford University could meet in a field, albeit an Oxford one, and still be the university. The English nation has been founded and formed by English speech; English speech has the power to transmit English values, and English values are given form by English poets. Poets such as Langland, Blake, Bunyan and Wordsworth who, in their own parochial landscapes, have found universal allegories to inspire the nation. As the ideas of farmers, translated into speech and thus to action, result in the draining of fenland, the diversion of streams, the construction of walls and dykes and all the myriad manifestations which are the physical landscape, so the ideas of poets and artists give form to the English soul, a soul which is a stony ground for the seedlings of tyranny, oppression or revolution.

This book is based on the writings of those who have brought light to the forest floor, the woodmen of language, law and religion. Through their coppicing they have brought into being a nation of individuals who do not have to fight for survival or struggle under oppressive ideology, individuals who may freely co-exist in a land under their own stewardship.

CONSIDER ENGLAND

DEDICATED TO
LEON MACLAREN AND
SHEILA ROSENBERG

THE ENGLAND WE SEE

He is fortunate who can
find an ideal England of
the past, the present and
the future to worship,
and embody it in his
native fields and waters,
or his garden, as in a
graven image.

EDWARD THOMAS:
The South Country

The Windrush Valley;
Swinbrook, Oxfordshire

13

Yes, I remember when the changeful earth,
And twice five summers on my mind had stamped
The faces of the moving year, even then
I held unconscious intercourse with beauty
Old as creation, drinking in a pure
Organic pleasure from the silver wreaths
Of curling mist, or from the level plain
Of waters coloured by impending clouds.

WILLIAM WORDSWORTH: The Prelude

 Between the departure of one vicar and the arrival of his replacement, a small parish church in England was left to the care of the villagers. An old man devoted himself to the overgrown vicarage garden and, by the time of the new vicar's arrival, it had become a garden of great beauty. The vicar, exploring his new home, came across the old man weeding in the shrubbery. 'My good man,' he said, 'between you, you and God have made a great wonder here.' The old man straightened up. 'You should have seen it when he had it to himself,' he said gruffly.

England did not acquire its beauty naturally, but by the hand of man at work with the elements of creation. Left to itself, it would revert in time to wood and bog, heath and fen. The climate of Britain is unique. Though the islands share the same latitude as Labrador and Siberia, the land is warmed by the Gulf Stream and by westerly winds, giving mild winters, cool summers and plentiful rain. King Charles II observed, probably rightly, that there is hardly any other country where a man can work comfortably in the open air the whole year round.

A climate without extremes has created a land similarly moderate. There are no deserts in England. Mountains are few, the wilderness small. Compared to, say, the Namib desert or the Grand Canyon, any dramatics attempted by the scenery are amateurish. But minimal props are more than compensated for by the lighting. When it comes to that we are in the hands of a professional. Its subtleties, its constant soft changings, can cast a dozen emotional moods on one scene every day. To watch the shadows of clouds chase across the Cotswolds, or the sun light up the old brick of a Surrey wall, to see the leaves of a tree open in lime and fall in russet, is

Wells-next-the-Sea, Norfolk

to be the blessed witness of one of the best shows on earth. Mists we have in plenty, fog and drizzle. We have overcast days and days when the sun seems to stay in bed. We have weather as our favourite topic of conversation, and weather forecasters who cheerfully coin new words such as 'mizzle' and 'thorms'. But apart from occasional droughts and floods, the worst English weather is usually little more than inconvenient. Unpredictable it may be, but of one thing we may be sure, whatever it is, we will not have it for long.

A progress through England is one of gentle unfolding. There are no abrupt beginnings or endings to the landscape. The fenny flatness of East Anglia and its huge skies give way gradually to the hills and dales of the Midlands, which themselves become the steeper hills and dales of Yorkshire. One needs to be some way into a county before distinguishing a difference, which usually shows through the colour of the soil and the building materials of the rural churches. As Arthur Quiller-Couch describes it in *The Art of Writing*: 'I am journeying, say, in the West of England. I cross a bridge over a stream dividing Devon from Cornwall. These two counties, each beautiful in its way, are quite unlike in their beauty; yet nothing happened as I stepped across the brook, and for a mile or two or even ten I am aware of no change. Sooner or later that change will break upon the mind and I shall be startled, awakening suddenly to a land of altered features. But at what turn of the road this will happen, just how long the small multiplied impressions will take to break into surmise, into conviction – that nobody can tell.'

The directives of the European Commission and the British government aside, it is so easy to be a farmer in England that, for much of our history, that is what most of us have been. There is no need for large scale irrigation, nor for the protection of crops from hurricanes, earthquakes or sub-zero winters. We have, of course, had all these things, but in scant measure.

The last great drama of the climate was the ice-sheet which withdrew ten thousand years ago. At that time Britain was still joined to the Continent. As the ice retreated the bare soil was colonized by tundra vegetation and glacial plants. The warming of the latitude encouraged trees from the south to move in and their arrival coincided roughly with the final parting of Britain from the Continent; in fact, they arrived just in time. By 3000 BC the islands of Britain had their shape, were inhabited by neolithic peoples, were carpeted in the south with broad-leaved trees and in the north with birch and pine.

Although woodland is the natural vegetation of the islands, much of what woodland we have left is not the remnant of wilderness, but the product of the work of man. The first inhabitants of these islands found the place densely forested with pine, hazel, wych-elm, oak, lime and alder. The primeval wildwood covered two-thirds of the British Isles. The human colonizers arrived in the period of the New Stone Age. Coming from the Mediterranean and the Aegean, they would have had contact with ancient Egypt. These cultural invaders were the first of a series from southern Europe: throughout history wave after wave of Mediterranean influence has washed over these islands, to England's lasting benefit. These neolithic peoples were farmers and had the farmer's attitude towards the trees. They were a resource for building materials and for fuel. For that reason, as well as for the creation of grazing land, the trees were felled. The Bronze Age of c. 2000 BC coincided with a

The arboretum of Oxford University at Nuneham Courtenay

new climatic period and saw the introduction of the beech tree, which favours the chalk uplands of southern Britain.

In the next wave of immigration from the Continent, the Celts arrived about 500 BC, bringing with them the iron industry and metal tools. They came in three waves: the Goidels, the Brythons and the Belgae. With the arrival of each group, the earlier inhabitants were either enslaved or pushed westward, a pattern of conquest later to be repeated by the Anglo-Saxons. With the coming of the Celts, great expanses of the country came under cultivation. By the time that the next phase of Mediterranean invasion came, in the form of the Romans, the land had been largely cleared of the ancient wildwood, and woodlands were subject to management.

The Romans occupied Britain for four hundred years. The majority of their soldiers were drawn from central and northern Europe rather than from Italy. Their building programmes reflect their character: straightforward, disciplined and uncompromising. Square forts went up on a plan provided by headquarters in Rome; roads were laid to run straight regardless of terrain; villas were of the same design as those in sunny Italy. As for the British, at least those that came under Roman rule, according to Tacitus 'there was a gradual yielding to the attractions of vice – such as covered walks and baths and eloquent banquets. This in their ignorance they called civilization; but it was only a part of their enslavement.'

As repeated barbarian attacks on Rome struck at the heart of the Empire, Britain was abandoned and the garrisons withdrawn. The romanized British fought on alone against the Picts in the north, the Irish in the west and the Saxons in the east. One vigorous battle, under the leadership of a man called Artorius or Arthur,

The Anglo-Saxon village reconstructed on the archaeological site at West Stow, Suffolk

set back Saxon ambitions forty years, but the sun was setting on Britain and the British. When it rose again, it was on a place called England, the land of the Angles.

The land which the Anglo-Saxons acquired was fertile but, while continuing to be cultivated in some areas, in others it had fallen into neglect. These invaders were of Germanic rather than Mediterranean stock. They enslaved many of the Romano-British Celts, driving the rest into Cornwall, Westmoreland, Wales, and such extensive tracts of dense woodland as remained. It is in the Anglo-Saxon period, which spans the five hundred years after the departure of the Romans, that both England and the English countryside came into being.

The relationship between the English and the sea is ambivalent. The English may have arrived as pirates, but they have never really been the seafaring nation they like to think they are. Naval heroes like Drake and Raleigh had more in common with the pirate than the gentleman, and in the great age of seafaring in the seventeenth and eighteenth centuries, the crew was likely to have been press-ganged into service, as Pepys noted regretfully in his diary while serving as Clerk to the Navy Board. That Nelson's crew so faithfully did its duty reflects more on the quality of the officer class than on the treatment the crew enjoyed from its masters in the Admiralty. The Navy, periodically dismantled only to be hastily built up again, is often forgotten by the nation, except of course when there is trouble at sea, be it in the Falklands or in the fishing grounds. England's continuance may yet depend on her Navy. 'As before and since in her history,' Churchill remarked in relation to Trafalgar, 'the Royal Navy alone seemed to stand between the Island and national destruction.' Unless one lives in Hampshire, where naval officers and

Besides, to see poor patient labouring men and housekeepers, leaving poor wifes and families, taken up on a sudden by strangers, was very hard; and that without press-money, but forced against all law to be gone. It is a great tyranny.

SAMUEL PEPYS: Diary, 1 July 1666

... the cottages and houses came in little groups, some
up crooked lanes, hidden away by elms as if out of sight
in a cupboard, and some dotted along the brooks,
scattered so that, unless you had connected them all
with a very long rope, no stranger could have told which
belonged to the village and which did not. They drifted
into various tithings, and yet it was all the same place.
They were all thatched. It was a thatched village. This is
strictly accurate and strictly inaccurate, for I think there
were one or two tiled and one 'slated' and perhaps
a modern one slate. Nothing is ever quite rigid or
complete that is of man; all rules have a chip in them.

RICHARD JEFFRIES: My Old Village

seamen come ashore and have their homes, the Navy is something that happens out
there on the sea, that dubious element which on the whole the English prefer to
admire from the coast. Certainly Anglo-Saxon literature expresses fear rather than
love of the sea and it seems that, as soon as they arrived, the English were quick to
become landlubbers. It comes as a surprise to learn that, according to the Parker
Chronicle, in the summer of 875 'Alfred sailed out to sea with a fleet, and fought
against seven ships' companies, and captured one of them and put the others to
flight', or that he had ships built to his own design that were swifter, steadier and
higher than others. Until, that is, one learns that Alfred recruited his crew from
Frisia. If in Alfred we have the forerunner of the great naval commander, in those
Saxons who would not sail with him, we have the forerunners of reluctant English
sailors! The Danes were much happier on the sea than the English. To go *a-viking*
(raiding by sea) was the standard winter pastime of Scandinavian farmers. Despite
his brave attempt to battle with the Vikings on water, it was to be on land that
Alfred finally contained their threat.

Before the Vikings arrived, however, the English had had three hundred
years in which to clear the land for cultivation and to turn England into a pastoral
paradise. The cycle of the farming year for the Anglo-Saxon included as much wood
and scrub clearance as tilling, planting and harvesting. Those who yearn for the
simple life of the peasant may not have considered the callouses on the hands that
must daily do battle with deep-rooted saplings, bramble and gorse. Such is the
productivity of English soil that each moment's neglect brings its sprout of weeds,
and, near the wood's edge, those weeds tend to be of the tough thistle variety.

The home described by Laurie Lee in
'Cider With Rosie', Slad, Gloucestershire

The village to which our family had come was a scattering of some twenty to thirty houses down the south-east slope of a valley. The valley was narrow, steep, and almost entirely cut off; it was also a funnel for winds, a channel for the floods and a jungly, bird-crammed, insect-hopping sun-trap whenever there happened to be any sun. It was not high and open like the Windrush country, but had secret origins, having been gouged from the Escarpment by the melting ice-caps some time before we got there. The old flood-terraces still showed on the slopes, along which the cows walked sideways. Like an island, it was possessed of curious survivals – rare orchids and Roman snails; and there were chemical qualities in the limestone-springs which gave the women pre-Raphaelite goitres. The sides of the valley were rich in pasture and the crests heavily covered in beechwoods.

Living down there was like living in a bean-pod; one could see nothing but the bed one lay in. Our horizon of woods was the limit of our world. For weeks on end the trees moved in the wind with a dry roaring that seemed a natural utterance of the landscape. In winter they ringed us with frozen spikes, and in summer they oozed over the lips of the hills like layers of thick green lava. Mornings, they steamed with mist or sunshine, and almost every evening threw streamers above us, reflecting sunsets we were too hidden to see.

LAURIE LEE: Cider With Rosie

The Anglo-Saxon village consisted of a huddle of cottages surrounded by great fields. The fields were divided into strips belonging to the villagers, and parcels of strips, called *furlongs*, were demarcated by deep ditches and banks. The hollow ways and sunken lanes we still have were originally created by two neighbouring banks. The first villagers were farmers, and most farmers lived in villages. As the population of the village grew, so the fields were extended and more woodland had to be cleared. Fields which were cut directly from woodland may have been enclosed by hedges from the beginning, but the majority had no boundary other than, at most, a ditch and earth bank. Apart from the patterning of the strips, therefore, the fields themselves looked more like the great expanses that modern farming has created than the little hedged fields of English nostalgia.

From Anglo-Saxon times to the Middle Ages, three distinct types of village evolved. One had houses grouped around a village green, another had them strung out along a street. In the third the houses grew up in a haphazard and chaotic huddle. In *The Making of the English Landscape*, W. G. Hoskins says 'in the period between 450 and 1066, England became a land of villages'. Nearly all the villages which survive today originated in that period and were recorded for posterity in the Domesday Book. Many have disappeared. Some died a natural death due to poverty of the soil. Some were abandoned during epidemics of plague. Many were swallowed up by Cistercian granges or land enclosure. All those that survive, however, are likely to have been established before the Domesday Book was compiled in 1086.

Tall nettles cover up, as they have done
These many springs, the rusty harrow, the plough
Long worn out, and the roller made of stone:
Only the elm butt tops the nettles now.

This corner of the farmyard I like most:
As well as any bloom upon a flower
I like the dust on the nettles, never lost
Except to prove the sweetness of a shower.

EDWARD THOMAS: Tall Nettles

The Anglo-Saxon system of land tenure was perhaps the purest system of land-ownership and management that England has enjoyed. Though Anglo-Saxon society was hierarchical, there was no question of the fields belonging to anyone other than to those who worked them. Because of the paucity of written documentation, the hideage system is difficult to understand, but in essence it was a system of taxation related to the productivity of the land. Those who had poor land, or who had suffered flooding or drought, paid less tax than those who could obtain better yields with greater ease. Consequently for those who obtained poor yields on good land the tax was punitive; the tenant either had to work harder or to move away to a more marginal area where laziness and neglect were not so expensive.

The justice of the hideage system is a reflection of the harmony with the land that is enjoyed by a village-based society. Mining and large-scale farming does not figure in the history of the early English as it does in that of the Romans. The respect of the Anglo-Saxon for nature seems to have been more akin to that of the native American. To the Anglo-Saxon the relationship between work on the land and the production of wealth was obvious; today, with our middlemen and money-markets, we have lost sight of it.

The idea of a village, romantically dishevelled with tall nettles obscuring rusting tools, with ivy and vines invading walls, with chickens, geese and ducks laying eggs under bushes, with a snuffling pig or two and some feral cats, is the form of a longing buried deep in the English soul. It means home and it means freedom. It means that what you get at the end of the day depends on what you have put in: reward and labour are directly related to each other. It expresses that which is so

dear to the English: justice.

If the ideal ever existed as a popular reality, it came to an end in 1066. The Anglo-Saxon ceorl might have thought that it made little difference when, overnight, he became a villein. He still had to work all the hours of light, but suddenly it was possible to work and starve in a land of plenty. In losing his king he lost his land. It was still physically his; its clay and loam still stuck to his shoes and got under his fingernails, but the produce of it more or less belonged to the one calling himself 'the lord'. The feudal system provided two classes of society ready not so much to reap the rewards as simply to take them once the work of reaping had been done by the peasants. One was the military class which, in return for food, undertook to fight battles, even though most of the battles were not Everyman's but the king's. The other was the church. With the Normans had come the great abbeys, their vast estates, and abbots as lordly as any baron. Whether his lord wore a habit or armour meant little to the poor villein who had lost his fundamental freedom, which was the tenure of a patch of land sufficient to feed himself and his family.

Not only were the villeins of the open fields to suffer. Many others, particularly those making a living from coppicing, charcoal burning and other tree-based industries, and those subsisting on moor, heath and fen, suddenly found themselves subject to Forest Law. The word *forest* means 'outside', that is, land beyond the village or town; the original term was not synonymous with extensive, unbroken woodland. The Anglo-Saxons had no forests; forests came with William the Conqueror who desired long rides for his beloved sport of hunting. The main

Moccas Park,
Herefordshire, one of
the oldest surviving
deerparks in England

Skipton Castle, once home
to the Clifford family. The
yew tree in Conduit Court
was planted by Anne
Clifford in 1569

24

I fear those grey old men of Moccas, those grey, gnarled, low-browed, knock-kneed, bowed, bent, huge, strange, long-armed, deformed, hunchbacked, mis-shapen old men that stand waiting and watching century after century biding God's time with both feet in the grave and yet tiring down and seeing out generation after generation, with such tales to tell, as when they whisper them to each other in the midsummer nights, make the silver birches weep and the poplars and aspens shiver and the long ears of the hares and rabbits stand on end. No human hand set those oaks. They are 'the trees which the Lord hath planted'. They look as if they had been at the beginning and making of the world, and they will probably see its end.

THE REV. FRANCIS KILVERT:
Diary, 22 April 1876

distinction between forest and non-forest was the laws pertaining to the area. As the Anglo-Saxon Chronicle records, 'The king William set up great protection for deer and legislated to that intent, that whosoever should slay hart or hind should be blinded … he loved the high-deer as if he were their father'.

It is often said that, under the Normans, a third of the country was designated 'forest' but that huge figure, if true, relates to legal forest and certainly does not mean that a third of the country was wooded. Forest land remained under either common or private ownership: the king only owned the deer and the trees, but with the forest laws in the king's favour, the landlord for once became as oppressed as the commoner. The proliferation of royal forests was finally halted with the signing of Magna Carta in 1215. It was in this period that the stories of Robin Hood arose, but it is unlikely that poaching was a capital offence. The Forest Courts appear to have been much more interested in fines than blindings. Sherwood Forest, it should be noted, was – and remains – largely heathland.

Whereas the forests were open land, parks were surrounded by palings. The word 'park' means enclosure, and the first parks were natural woodland. Although most of the forests have gone, destroyed either by enclosure, neglect or Victorian mismanagement, many parks survive. Their tradition is longer and more enduring, and was reinvigorated by 'landscape gardeners' such as Capability Brown and William Kent. There are now, it seems, plans to reafforest England with trees, but the new forests will take hundreds of years to establish themselves, and some old opinions will have to be uprooted in the process. It is not unusual to hear someone muttering about ruin and damnation as a wood, suddenly coming back to life, begins

My aspens dear, whose airy cages quelled,
           Quelled or quenched in leaves the leaping sun,
    All felled, felled, are all felled;
                Of a fresh and following folded rank
                    Not spared, not one
                    That dandled a sandalled
              Shadow that swam or sank
On meadow and river and wind-wandering
           weed-winding bank.

       O if we but knew what we do
                When we delve or hew –
        Hack and rack the growing green!
             Since country is so tender
      To touch, her being so slender,
      That, like this sleek and seeing ball
      But a prick will make no eye at all,
      Where we, even where we mean
                To mend her we end her,
        When we hew or delve:
After-comers cannot guess the beauty been.
    Ten or twelve, only ten or twelve
      Strokes of havoc unselve
           The sweet especial scene,
     Rural scene, a rural scene,
     Sweet especial rural scene.

GERARD MANLEY HOPKINS: Binsey Poplars

to whir and creak with the sound of cutters; the sound, that is, of active management. The unspoilt, peaceful woodland is likely to be, in reality, a place of neglect and decay, whereas healthy countryside, under good stewardship, echoes with the sound of men at work.

Forests, parks, woodlands: all depend on that which is most beloved of the English, the tree. The very names of trees are music to the English ear: rowan, alder, elm, service, beech, birch, holly, hornbeam; but the king of them all is the oak. The oak that was the scene of Anglo-Saxon village councils became the oak nibbled by the king's deer, became the oak that provided the timber for the great ships. The woods were so depleted by events such as the Spanish Armada that in 1664 the diarist John Evelyn went round the country persuading landowners to plant trees, millions of them according to his own account. Ironically they came to fruition just in time to serve the needs of the navy in the Napoleonic Wars.

The English are far more likely to become passionate about the fate of a tree than about that of a stone monument. *Forum* and *forest* share the same etymological root, but do not share the same emotive force in the English breast. 'Old trees,' said Oliver Rackham in *The History of the Countryside*, 'though uncommon, are a speciality of England. Europe is a continent of young or youngish trees, like a human population with compulsory euthanasia at age thirty; one can go from Boulogne to Athens without seeing a tree more than 200 years old.'

Tree-lore, tree-culture and tree-worship provide a vital connection in spirit between the Anglo-Saxon and the Celt, both of which peoples performed religious rites in sacred groves. If the Anglo-Saxons chose to build in logs, wattle, daub and

Old Romney, Kent

reeds, the choice was deliberate: their continental connections were extensive and they knew well enough about the arts of masonry. For a long time it has been assumed that their humble huts were an indication of primitiveness. Each society, however, has its motivating ideas, and if one of them is that each new family should have a new house, that to live in anyone else's house is a mark of poverty, building in stone will have nothing to recommend it. Stone is an expensive, intractable material, difficult to demolish. Just as to a modern Indian the English idea of taking a bath by lying prone in stagnant water is repugnant, so may the Anglo-Saxon have viewed the idea of living in a house once lived in by others. There was only one who would live long enough to warrant the effort of building in stone, and that was God. Thus, with the coming of Christianity, the wooden villages which merged with the landscape began to feature a stone-built chapel.

There was plenty of quarried stone to be had if the village was close to a ruined Roman camp or villa. Escombe chapel, near Durham, which has seen almost continuous worship since the seventh century, was built of stone from the ruins of Vinovium (Binchester). At Escombe we find tangible proof that the Anglo-Saxons spurned rather than merely ignored Roman culture: any masonry block with a Latin inscription was deliberately placed upside down. The Anglo-Saxons believed that words had magical properties; they also believed that Roman culture was synonymous with corruption, and so they upturned their inscriptions to rob them of their power.

The stone churches of the carpenter-race tended to be heavy and graceless. The fine tradition of English churches built by masons with local stone, granite,

The chancel arch in the Anglian church at Escomb, Co. Durham, was a Roman arch plundered from a ruined fort at nearby Binchester

27

Little Rollright,
Oxfordshire

limestone or flint, begins in the twelfth century under the influence of the Normans. Whether the churches had spires or not depended on the quality of the local materials. Generally, spires are a good indication of being in the limestone belt and Northamptonshire is the great county of the spired church. There were other considerations which determined the architecture. In Herefordshire and Shropshire, which are close to the Welsh border, and therefore to the Welsh, the churches were given defensive towers. Spires were the first man-made features to make a contrast with nature but, being made of local materials, that contrast was harmonious.

During the Anglo-Saxon period little had happened to the landscape other than the foundation of villages, the creation of a few parks, and a lot of tidying up. With the Normans came their deer and the forests. Their reclamation of marsh and fen created the familiar landscape of willow-lined ditches, rich green pastures and scattered farmsteads, but none of these things effected a change that was noticeable in the timespan of one generation. True, castles joined the churches on the skyline, but the land itself looked much the same as before. The thing which was to alter the view dramatically was the humble sheep.

By the fourteenth century the economy of Europe had become dominated by the bearers of wool. The wool trade linked the fates of England, Flanders, France and Italy. Men grew rich on the fruits of trade, built new houses on its profits, and formed a new class of society called the middle- or merchant-class. The best wool came from English sheep; the best weaving was done in Flanders; the best dyeing and finishing was done in Italy. The stresses of this radical change in the economy challenged the system of feudalism and was a direct cause of the Hundred Years

War. To tour the Cotswolds, that rolling, benign landscape which is God's gift to sheep, is to walk through the history of the wool trade. From the stone grandeur of Painswick houses to the wool-bale tombs of Burford, the whole area is a monument to one resource.

It was not only the new wealth that created visible change. Sheep require pasture, and it was had at the cost of the open fields and the people that worked them. Large areas of arable land were cleared and turned over to grazing. To pen the sheep, the land was fenced.

'There is nothing good nor bad but thinking makes it so,' said Shakespeare and there is nothing quite like thinking about the history of the enclosures to bother the English and even more so the Scots. Those to whom good and bad are absolutes see enclosure as badness writ large. The first period of enclosures, in Tudor times, had men of the stature of Thomas More and Francis Bacon making vehement protest. The depopulation of the land to make way for sheep was, they said, an injustice, as was the enclosure of land which, for centuries, had been held in common by villagers for the pasturing of their horses and cattle.

Undoubtedly some Tudor landlords abused ancient laws of custom, but the sum total of their sins was small compared to what was to come. Until the Restoration, successive governments resisted petitions from private landlords for large-scale enclosure. Then in 1750 Parliament gave its assent. The changes then wrought upon the landscape were rapid and dramatic: suddenly a man could see his surroundings as it were completely redrawn and repainted. Large fields and open heaths, lanes winding alongside natural boundaries, were covered with a regular

Wool-bale tombs, Swinbrook, Oxfordshire

Swamps of wild rush-beds and slough's squashy traces,
Grounds of rough fallows and thistle and weed,
Flats and low vallies of kingcups and daisies,
Sweetest of subjects are ye for my reed:
Ye commons left free in the rude rags of nature,
Ye brown heaths beclothed in furze as ye be,
My wild eye in rapture adores every feature,
Ye are dear as this heart in my bosom to me.

O native endearments! I would not forsake ye,
I would not forsake you for sweetest of scenes:
For sweetest of gardens that nature could make me
I would not forsake ye, dear valleys and greens:
Thou Nature ne'er dropped ye a cloud-resting mountain,
Nor waterfalls tumble their music so free,
Had Nature denied ye a bush, tree or fountain,
Ye still had been loved as an Eden by me.

JOHN CLARE: The Village Minstrel

chequerboard of hedged enclosures. In the Midlands particularly the countryside was utterly transformed in two or three years.

The monotonous squareness of the new fields must have offended the eye used to natural variety. The fields were marked out initially by a ditch and earthbank on which was planted quickset hawthorn. With the farmers now divorced from their place of work, they quit the villages to build remote and isolated homesteads in the middle of their fields. Between 1750 and 1850, two-and-a-half thousand Acts of Parliament licensed the enclosure of four million acres of land, affecting three thousand parishes. All those single-track lanes we see running off A roads and B roads at ninety degrees, leading to hamlets and farms, come from the drastic reorganization of the countryside which took place in one hundred years.

It is said that in the eighteenth century England achieved fruition. All the land that could be cultivated was in cultivation, and the rural life was simple and idyllic. Most of our folklore and folk imagery derives from this period, the time of the pastoral paradise which Constable captured in his paintings. But as rural life flowered, so it died. In redrawing all the boundaries, enclosure displaced thousands of peasants. In Scotland, the dispossessed were driven to the ports and emigration ships. In England, they were driven to the towns and factories.

The enormous changes of the eighteenth century had begun a hundred years earlier. With the Restoration, Parliament curbed the powers of the monarch and increased its own. Between 1688 and 1760, the Houses of Parliament and local bodies of administration had a common purpose: the advancement of the interests of the land-owning aristocracy. The yeoman farmer, that son of the emancipated

*Hawthorn hedges
today tend to be cut
back severely in spring
but some are left to
grow tall and to flower*

villein, the stalwart example of independence, the free man who was the very creation of the Common Law, who could sit on juries and represent his shire in Parliament, was overtaken by the great landowner and his great country house. Of all the losses suffered in English history, the annihilation of the yeoman is perhaps the one to be most regretted. With the small-holdings gone, the craftsmen reduced to landless labourers, and the villages deserted, that land-owning aristocracy was free to have its rolling acres landscaped 'naturally' by William Kent or Capability Brown and to have the new parkland set off by a romantic ruin.

But there is nothing good nor bad .... Yesterday's evil can sometimes prove to be today's good, for who now is not enamoured of the hawthorn hedges, many of which are two hundred or more years old? – hawthorn hedges, which provide miles of snowy blossom in spring, which are home to a wealth of wildlife, which ribbon the land into so many little parcels. The voice of protest which sounded at their setting sounds again at their grubbing up. The national conscience once troubled by the displacement of peasants is now disturbed by the eviction of sparrows and woodmice. The John Clare who bemoaned the loss of his heath is now the Suffolk lad alarmed by the replacement of his fields with wheaten prairies. England has the greatest diversity of wildlife in the world, and much of it has arrived and flourished as a *result* of man's work upon the land, including hedge-laying. It is difficult to see the good in present farming policies, but who knows but that one day it might not become evident?

Enclosure had another hidden grace which took a while to be discovered. The extent of enclosure rested on the ownership of the land. Where it was owned

Port Meadow, a long stretch of common land in Oxford, administered by the Sheriff, where citizens may graze cattle and horses

by one landlord, the act of enclosure was straightforward, but where a parish was under mixed ownership, it could only be effected by sale or exchange. Common land which was used for pasturage remained in many places, and the rights to it might be manifold. When the new industrial towns began to grow, their spread depended on the easy acquisition of surrounding fields, and common land was far more difficult to acquire than enclosed land. Urban sprawl is no good thing, but far worse is urban overpopulation. The inhuman crowding of people into squalid tenements in Nottingham in the nineteenth century was in part caused by the town being surrounded by common land with disputed rights. In a Nottinghamshire village called Laxton a dispute on enclosure rights was never resolved, with the consequence that today Laxton is still surrounded by open fields worked in the medieval manner.

For most of its history, England has fought shy of urban life. The English inherited a land that had been civilized by the Romans and, for the most part, were happy to let the towns fall into neglect. These were not towns as we know them today but merely groups of huts surrounded by an earthen bank, one town linked to another by a road. The Anglo-Saxons found the roads useful but nonetheless sited their villages well away from them. According to Tacitus, writing on the Germanic peoples of the first century AD, they 'regarded towns as the defence of slavery and the grave of freedom' and it may be that the Saxons brought the same idea with them when they moved into Britain.

The towns abandoned by the Romans began to revive when the Anglo-

Saxons were converted to Christianity. The first bishops, when choosing sites for their cathedrals, were predisposed towards old Roman towns such as London, York and Canterbury. For similar reasons monasteries chose such sites as Gloucester and Bath. But it was the coming of the Vikings in the ninth century that created the English town.

The Vikings arrived in the same fashion as the English before them had done, first in small raiding parties, then in hosts of settlers. They were keener on urban life than the Anglo-Saxon, however, and followed in the fort-building tradition of the Iron-Age Celts and the Romans. Faced with the organized armies and strong defences of the Vikings, the Anglo-Saxon farmers were forced to respond in kind and, under the leadership of Alfred the Great, adopted the tactics not only of Scandinavian defence but also of Scandinavian discipline. Hitherto warfare had been on the level of skirmishes between the various tribal kingdoms of Northumberland, Mercia, Wessex, Essex, Kent and Sussex. Now it involved strategic planning, and the common enemy presented by the Vikings was a major element in the forging of the English into a single nation.

Another was the personality of the king. Alfred is the only king to have been called 'Great' by the English. The reasons for this will become evident as we discover time and again that, as Abraham stands in the history of the Jews, so does Alfred stand at the beginning of the English nation. The wars with the Vikings had almost killed the fledgling nation before it could properly fly. Within a hundred years the Anglo-Saxons, who had been foremost in European scholarship, had become illiterate and, by 878, were on the point of being completely overwhelmed.

What shall I say of the cities and towns that he [Alfred] restored, and of the others he had built where none stood before? Of the buildings marvellously wrought with gold and silver under his direction. Of the royal halls and chambers, wonderfully built of stone and wood at his command.

ASSER: Life of Alfred the Great

The site of Alfriston, East Sussex, has been continuously occupied since at least Roman times

The great kingdoms of East Anglia, Mercia and Northumberland had already fallen to the Vikings – only Wessex remained. At the lowest point in his fortunes, Alfred hid with his men in the peat bogs of the Somerset levels, with their camp on the small marsh island of Athelney. For a year or so Athelney, which is about the size of Trafalgar Square, was the English nation. Then everything changed. We do not know how or why but perhaps in a psychological conflict akin to arm-wrestling, as Alfred fought back, so his enemy Guthram crumpled. The end came with Guthram's conversion to Christianity – he was baptised by Alfred – and in a treaty which divided the country between the north-east (the Danelaw) and the south-west (Wessex).

It was in order to strengthen Wessex that Alfred created thirty-three *burhs*, or fortified towns. They were so arranged as to be only a day's march from each other. Some were old Roman towns such as Bath, Winchester and Chichester, others were Iron Age forts such as that at Uffington. Some like Wareham, Cricklade and Wallingford, were new forts established on rectangular plots. With these creations Alfred was instituting urban life in England and had to assign men to living in them as a form of duty.

The creation of the *burhs* was based on the hideage system which had served Anglo-Saxon farmers so well. 'If every hide is represented by one man, then every pole of wall can be manned by four men.' By this reckoning, twenty-seven thousand men were conscripted in a scheme of defence over thirty-three *burhs*. And the length of the walls in each *burh* corresponds to the formula of the Burghal Hideage.

The *burhs* were founded as forts but, after the Vikings had been settled in the

*Stokesay Castle,
Shropshire*

eastern territory called the 'Danelaw', the potential of the *burhs* as trading centres began to be assessed. Some were abandoned, others developed and Anglo-Saxon laws demanded that trade should take place in them. A German arrangement of the same time, which may have provided the English with a model, stipulated that every ninth 'agrarian soldier' was to live in a town and build dwellings for his eight colleagues, who were to keep him supplied, and to hold councils, meetings and parties in the town, 'that they might learn in peace what they would have to do in emergency against enemies'.

If the foundation of towns over southern England was the product of Alfred's vision, it was left to later kings to determine their future. Many of the towns became mints and paid profitable rents to the king. Up until the thirteenth century, they remained under royal jurisdiction, governed by the king's sheriff. Then to pay for the Crusades Richard I and King John realized some capital by selling the towns their freedom. With the granting of the royal charters the towns were able to choose their own officials, to charge tolls, issue licences for market and to hold courts. Power and wealth began to devolve to merchants and tradesmen and the enterprising and the ambitious among the rural population were drawn to urban life. To cope with the expansion, many new towns were founded in the thirteenth century by royal decree.

With the wool and wine trade flourishing, fortunes were to be made and rising men of the middle class spent their profits on country estates and house-building. Lawrence of Ludlow, for example, was the son of a clothier. He did so well in the wool trade that eventually he built himself a castle. Stokesay is

*The Guildhall at Much
Wenlock, Shropshire, built
in 1577 over the original
medieval 'lock-up', served
until recently as a Court
Room and still hosts
monthly meetings of
the Town Council*

When soothing darkness spreads
O'er hill and vale, and the punctual stars,
While all things else are gathering to their homes,
Advance, and in the firmament of heaven
Glitter – but undisturbing, undisturbed;
As if their silent company were charged
With peaceful admonitions for the heart
Of all-beholding Man, earth's thoughtful lord;
Then, in full many a region, once like this
The assured domain of calm simplicity
And pensive quite, an unnatural light
Prepared for never-resting labour's eyes
Breaks from a many-windowed fabric huge;
And at the appointed hour a bell is heard,
Of harsher import than the curfew-knoll

That spake the Norman Conqueror's stern behest –
A local summons to unceasing toil!
Disgorged are now the Ministers of day;
And, as they issue from the illumined pile,
A fresh band meets them, at the crowded door –
And in the courts – and where the rumbling stream,
That turns the multitude of dizzy wheels,
Glares, like a troubled spirit, in its bed,
Among the rock below. Men, maidens, youths,
Mother and little children, boys and girls,
Enter, and each the wonted task resumes
Within his temple, where is offered up
To Gain, the master idol of the realm,
Perpetual sacrifice.

WILLIAM WORDSWORTH: The Excursion

The windpower station
at Shore, West Yorkshire

Nothing can make me believe that the present condition of your Black Country yonder is an unchangeable necessity of your life and position: such miseries as this were begun and carried on in pure thoughtlessness, and a hundredth part of the energy that was spent in creating them would get rid of them.

WILLIAM MORRIS: The Beauty of Life

significant in two respects. One is that it materially represents the new class of the English gentry; the other that it is one of the first castles built as a home rather than a fort. As a defensible home rather than a residential fortress, it marks the transitional stage in English society from a warring nation to a trading one.

The English gentry, the knights of the shire and the yeomen farmers became the backbone of the English Parliament. From Anglo-Saxon times the king had been accustomed to taking the advice of councillors in the *witangemot*. The Norman kings did the same, following the French model of *parlement*. It was during the baronial revolt of Simon de Montfort in the thirteenth century that the base of the council was broadened to include representatives of the towns and shires. Later, when Parliament was established by Edward I, the writ to the sheriffs summoned 'four knights from among those knights of your county who are more discreet and law worthy, and likewise from each of the cities, boroughs, and market towns of your bailiwick, six or four citizens, burgesses or other good men'.

The formation and growth of a town depended on certain elements being present in its sizing. One of the most important was that vital artery of trade, the river. Crossings were natural places for towns to grow up and, in time, fords and ferries became replaced by bridges. Even though it may have spelt the difference between a town thriving or dying, for centuries the presence of a well-maintained bridge depended on the generosity of local benefactors.

Watermills first appeared in the Middle Ages to harness the energy of the rivers, but it was when that energy was applied to machinery that factories became additional features to the landscape. The first of them were built near a falling

36

Meanwhile, at social Industry's command,
How quick, how vast an increase! From the germ
Of some poor hamlet, rapidly produced
Here a huge town, continuous and compact,
Hiding the face of earth for leagues – and there,
Where not a habitation stood before,
Abodes of men irregularly massed
Like trees in forests, – spread through spacious tracts,
O'er which the smoke of unremitting fires
Hangs permanent, and plentiful as wreaths
Of vapour glittering in the morning sun.
And, wheresoe'r the traveller turns his steps,
He sees the barren wilderness erased,
Or disappearing …

WILLIAM WORDSWORTH: The Excursion

The back-to-backs at
Skipton, Yorkshire

stream to be close to their source of power. Their siting in secluded valleys also helped them to evade inspection and regulation. The first factory-owners built themselves proud halls near their rural factories but these were soon engulfed by the industrial wastelands they helped to create.

The invention of steam power in the early nineteenth century enabled manufacturers to leave the dales and site themselves by newly-constructed canals by which coal was being transported. In the towns streets of terraced housing were rapidly constructed, often by wily speculators on morbid land wisely left vacant by earlier generations. The word 'slum' comes from 'slump', meaning wet mire. If the land was wet to begin with, with difficult drainage problems it became wetter and the sanitary conditions were soon appalling. Sometimes the new housing was built 'back-to-back', that is, the backyards faced other backyards across a cobbled alley, while fronts faced fronts. Gardens were not included in the plans. In response to the alternative of tower block housing, however, terraces and back-to-backs have recently assumed a desirability that would have staggered their original occupants.

Following the enslavement of the factory workers came the charitable foundations established to relieve their lot. The industrial towns became the scenes of religious revival. Nonconformist congregations formed, built chapels and meeting houses. Altruistic projects followed: schools, hospitals, parks, public libraries.

The new industrial towns often grew out of hamlets. In the 1830s there was a single farmhouse near the banks of the Tees. Fifty years later, and now called Middlesborough, it was a vast expanse of terraces and factories housing more than fifty thousand people.

Bedford Square, London

 England's economic division into north and south was determined by its geology. While the agriculturally rich southern half built up its beautiful county towns, the land of the north, which was crop-poor and coal-rich, was hit by industrial blight. Benefactors and philanthropists did much to invest Liverpool, Manchester, Leeds, Sheffield and Nottingham with civic dignity, but the resentment seeded in the north by the abuses of the industrial revolution has not been salved yet. There is a belief among the English that any city which is not London is, at best, second rate.

Partly for this reason, London is full of people. It has a population of nearly seven million (almost the same as Paris, which is the capital of a country over twice the size of the United Kingdom). Founded in Roman times it was not until after the Great Fire in the seventeenth century that it began to develop into one of the largest cities in the world. It grew up as two centres, the City of London and the City of Westminster which, until comparatively recently, were separated by fields. Though the two have now merged, their functions are still distinct, with the City of London the centre of trade and the City of Westminster the administrative centre of the United Kingdom. Within the bounds of Westminster are Buckingham Palace, Westminster Abbey, the Houses of Parliament, Downing Street and the various governmental offices of Whitehall, while the City of London includes the Bank of England, the Stock Exchange and all the great financial institutions. With the pressure of building London began to spread into the home counties. Middlesex, the territory of the Middle Saxons which once included London, has now almost been taken over by its cuckoo baby. Much of Essex, the territory of the East Saxons,

The river Avon, Bath

has gone the same way. Hertfordshire, Buckinghamshire and Surrey have managed to maintain their distance but northern Kent, like southern Essex, has become the overspill homeland of that native of the East End, the Cockney. To look at a map of the country is to see the arterial network of roads converging on the heart which is London. The coming of television and radio exacerbated the division between the capital and the rest of the country and, despite the efforts made by local broadcasting, much is still capital-centred.

It was in London in the 1630s that high class residential areas were introduced, an idea that had come from Italy. Covent Garden, Bloomsbury Square, St. James's Square and Soho Square grew up quickly. Bedford Square was laid out in 1775 on land still largely agricultural and within fifty years Bloomsbury had sprung up and was housing nearly seventy thousand. The concept of squares and three-storey terraced houses of grand design was the product of the seventeenth and eighteenth centuries and gave rise to Bath, Buxton, Tunbridge Wells, Cheltenham and Leamington Spa, all of them created as health resorts for London-based society.

It is only in the last hundred and fifty years that England has become a truly urban society. If 'civilization' depends on living in cities, England came to it late and France has not got there yet. Both nations are agrarian in spirit. The great civilizations of Greece and Rome were founded on cities and their modern heirs are indifferent to many of the matters that fire a Saxon or Gallic heart. The French still enjoy a strong rural society, but the English lost theirs in the industrial revolution.

For most English people, to live in a large industrial town or city is a necessity rather than a choice. The young enjoy city life but with age comes the

Going up such a road, between steep banks of chalk and the roots and projecting bases of beeches whose foliage meets over-head – a road worn twenty feet deep, and now scarce ever used as a footpath except by fox and hare – we may be half-conscious that we have climbed that way before during the furrowing of the road, and we move as in a dream between this age and that dim one which we vainly strive to recover.

EDWARD THOMAS: The South Country

longing to leave, to return to the country. If English roads are clogged with traffic, it is because for most it is not possible to live and work in the same place. There are houses in the villages and there is work in the cities. Over the years the suburbs have arisen as a compromise, but they still entail travel.

The industrial revolution divorced the English from the land, but they kept what freedoms they could. Footpaths and rights of way, established in ancient times, are protected today by ramblers pounding their way through fields, often on paths which are only visible on the maps of the Ordnance Survey. The Ramblers Association, a name which once conjured images of harmless walkers with rucksacks and woolly hats, is beginning to assume a more belligerent reputation. Ramblers sometimes seem to be the last warriors in a battle that was lost centuries ago, but they are keeping alive those rights of access which remain.

Divorced from the land, and with country walks reduced to marked ways, the English have had to create their own edens. More than any other nation, England is possessed by the ideal of owning your own plot. The Englishman's home is his castle, and, any castle worthy of its name must have a garden.

The Anglo-Saxon vegetable plot (Old English *leac-ton* or 'leek patch') became a garden in the eleventh century, under the influence of the monks. The monastic walled garden, devoted to medicinal plants and culinary herbs, created a trend soon followed by individual households. The first towns were spacious enough to allow for gardens and orchards within the town walls, and even in the

40

City of London each house had its own kitchen garden. The first public pleasure gardens, created for 'refreshment of the senses' appeared in the twelfth century.

The grid pattern of the medieval garden was determined by the drainage systems but in time the straightforward geometry was elaborated and the short clipped hedges took more circuitous routes to meet each other. With the gardens of the Elizabethan age came the quincunx knot as a symbol of Englishness, though not for the first time, for it was the intricate knot, symbolic both of eternity and the inter-relatedness of creation, which was the basis of both Celtic and Anglo-Saxon art. Elizabethan gardens were richly symbolic, not only in the patterns of planting but also in the choice of plants themselves. A tricoloured pansy might represent the three Graces, or nine flowers in a knot the Virtues. Though the garden enjoyed a revival throughout Europe in the sixteenth century, such emblematic planting was peculiar to England.

Following the Romans and Christianity, the next wave of Mediterranean influence to sweep over northern Europe and England was the Renaissance. It brought with it a Latin purified of medieval degeneration, the Latin of the classical poets rather than the early fathers, and the English language, always ready to increase its vocabulary, became greatly enlarged with words of Latin and Greek derivation. As the vocabulary of the language multiplied, so the plant lists of gardeners increased dramatically with foreign borrowings. Explorations in the Far East and in the New World resulted in a stream of new garden accessions. In the seventeenth century, John Tradescant went abroad expressly to find plants in the nurseries of Europe but it was his son who began the more exotic tradition of plant-

The Temperate House,
Kew Gardens, Surrey

hunting, going off to Spain and North Africa on a ship bound in pursuit of pirates, and bringing back apricots and lilacs.

The botany boom caught the interest of Frederick, Prince of Wales, and his wife Augusta. A part of their land by the Thames at Kew became the basis of the Royal Botanic Garden. It was not the first garden set up for the scientific study of plants. That was in Padua. Even in England Kew was preceded by the Oxford Botanic Garden and the Chelsea Physick Garden. But these were founded to pursue knowledge of medicine whereas Kew was founded to pursue knowledge of plants. Within thirty years it had nearly six thousand species on its plant list and today it is, unofficially, the world centre for botanical studies.

Kew's collectors went everywhere in search of specimens. Sir Joseph Hooker, himself a director of Kew, brought back twenty-seven species of rhododendron from the Himalayas. Not all the plants acquired were for the ornamentation of English gardens: many species were transferred from one continent to another in the cause of developing colonial agriculture. Even the humblest English garden, however, became a beneficiary of the hard endeavours of the botanists.

Along with new plants came new garden designs. George Herbert's stepfather, John Danvers, is credited with the introduction of the Italian style of formal layout conducive to philosophic reflection. His garden at Chelsea attracted men such as John Donne and the Lord Chancellor, Sir Francis Bacon. Before long much of the aristocracy was laying out gardens in the Italian or French style. Renaissance exuberance froze into Puritan formality, a formality which reached its starkest limits with the rigid vistas introduced by William of Orange. The history of

gardening moves likes a pendulum between the formal and the informal design and the regimented lines of formality were swept away by William Kent, whose designed landscapes followed nature's rules. At the same time as the English began to tire of the *parterre*, they had new plants to accommodate: magnolias from China, japonicas from Japan, choisyas from Mexico, fuchsias from South America, hollyhocks from Arabia, poppies from India and the ivy-leaved geranium from South Africa. These and other such blowsy plants resist the tight embrace of clipped privet and box preferring freedom and luxurious abandon.

The finest contemporary gardens seek a balance between the formal and informal, between architectural design and natural abundance. At his Highgrove home in Gloucestershire the Prince of Wales has turned a bleak, unimaginative estate into a plantsman's paradise. One garden opens on to another, each embraced warmly by a wall or hedge, each containing plants individually selected for their colour, scent or form. The success of this garden rests on a subtle understanding of shape and design. While the productive part of the estate, Home Farm, experiments with organic farming methods, the Highgrove gardens are dedicated simply to natural beauty. As with the first gardens conceived by man, they refresh the senses and invite repose.

The tulips standing proud in the meadow, the honesty at the base of every tree in the drive, the pleached hornbeams, the fragrant balsam trees, the espalier apples bending over backwards to form arches in attitudes of supreme generosity – all the plants at Highgrove have a sense of duty. The combined effect of colour and form, the contrast between formal and informal, native and foreign (particularly

To me one of the great privileges of being lucky enough to be involved in the management of land, or in the development of a garden is to invest in the future; to create features in the landscape which in due course may strike a chord in the hearts of our descendants.

HRH The Prince of Wales: from the introduction to Highgrove – Portrait of an Estate

Levens Hall, Cumbria, home of the Bagot family. The topiary gardens were first laid out in 1694

Italian and Japanese) elements, create harmony. The very air is gentle. Plants do not merely grow and increase at Highgrove: they stand as evidence that, when man and nature work together, the result is art.

A study of the history of English horticulture shows the same forces at work which have shaped the English language: a native stock, greatly enhanced by foreign borrowings, with those borrowings undergoing a process of assimilation so complete that foreignness is removed. Today the non-native plants outnumber the native in vast proportion but many have become so essentially English that their exotic origins are quite forgotten. Who is now aware that the apple came from Palestine, the runner bean from Guatemala, the strawberry from North America, and the cucumber from India?

Plants from other climates require work to make them grow here. Soils have to be adjusted, hardier types of plant cultivated and, in many cases, temperatures controlled. With the exotic plants came the greenhouses and the conservatories such as the Palm House at Kew. The dedication of the English to gardens and gardening is undinted by the amount of work that has to be put in to make things grow in the English climate and soil. It is a devotion that can easily tip into eccentricity and obsession.

While botanic gardens are the repositories of wild species, the collection of cultivars is as much the work of the amateur as the professional. In 1979, to co-ordinate the work of both institutions and private individuals, the National Council for the Conservation of Plants and Gardens was set up. Its aim is to maintain and conserve all known garden plants. Within ten years there were four hundred collections listed and the range of collectors has proved as diverse as the plants. While, as one might expect, the Royal Horticultural Society gardens at Wisley foster several collections, and the Ministry of Agriculture looks after apples, it is the Brighton Parks and Gardens Department which has the lilacs, and two ladies of Huish, near Bristol, who have the michaelmas daisies. The collection of lychnis is in the care of the children of Hinchley Wood School in Esher, Surrey, while the Prince of Wales looks after the National Collection of beech trees. It can all seem mildly dotty, and not only to foreigners, but when it comes to gardens and gardening there is little that the English do not know.

Every town has its allotments, provided to compensate for the loss of common land and the lack of gardens in the industrial cities. They were originally sited on the edge of town but, with urban expansion, they have sometimes become quite central, yet these shabby fields are so sacred that no one dares suggest that they might be prime building sites. Organized on the ancient strip system, rented in measures of poles for a nominal fee, the allotment is the closest one can truly get to merry old England. Bent double amongst the cabbage patches and onion sets, the beanpoles and the wonky sheds, men and women labour to produce food they could buy more cheaply at the market. But nothing, they claim, has the flavour of the homegrown. This is perhaps the nearest they can get to expressing the inexpressible but, if there are such things as folk memories, they are surely released in a flood when battling against the slug and the snail, side by side with your neighbour on your cultivated strip. After a generation of decline, allotments are enjoying a renaissance of enthusiasm and are becoming as multi-cultural as the city centres.

Next to the cabbages one might find Italian plum tomatoes or peppers or African yams: the merry English habit of being home to all nations and all things is flourishing by the side of the canal and the railway embankment.

The Horticultural Society was formed in a Piccadilly bookshop in 1804. The first exhibit ever was a potato but today the Society, now designated 'Royal', plays host to thousands of visitors in the grounds of the Chelsea Hospital each May. Under the awning of a marquee the size of St Pancras railway station, proud growers display flowers that seem ambitious to attain to the Platonic Ideal. If the Chelsea Flower Show is famed throughout the world, so is the humbler version, the village show, but not for the same reason. Where Chelsea exemplifies the aspiration towards eternal beauty, the village show is associated with the aspiration towards infernal size. It began in the nineteenth century with gooseberry shows. The wild gooseberry is sour and it took the work of generations of gardens, from the sixteenth century to the nineteenth, to selectively cultivate the sweet fruit of English summer puddings. Easy to grow in the back-to-backs of the industrial Midlands and north, it excited competition between the growers. The competition was matched by co-operation, and the result was that by the end of the nineteenth century there were two thousand varieties in cultivation. The contest extended to other fruits and vegetables and before long the nation's gardeners were dedicating themselves to the production of the shortest, thickest pot leek, the longest carrot, the heaviest onion. The fever to produce these fancies, fanned by *The Guinness Book of Records*, is now international. Foolish it might be, but it still exemplifies the English attitude towards cultivation: no trouble is too much.

Current attitudes do not smile upon these products of obvious artificiality and the monster marrow may soon become extinct. The ethics of ecology are causing other shifts in fashion. The native plants, yesterday's weeds, are today's 'wildflowers' and, while one generation is still pulling them up, another is beginning to put them in.

The formal *parterre* was swept away by Capability Brown and William Kent. The knot returned in Victorian times. A fashion for bedding-out in patterns came, and should have gone again, except that municipal parks departments became peculiarly wedded to them. Over the centuries, we have tried every kind of garden, but the one that springs to mind with the words 'English garden' is lush, fragrant and has a wildness that belies the work that has gone into it. It surrounds a thatched cottage, is crowded with hollyhocks and lupines and old-fashioned roses of subtle, pastel shades. It is a garden to wade through like a meadow, full of scent and bees. The formal gardens of great houses, designed by architects and clipped by machines, draw many visitors but few try to repeat at home what they have seen. The keenest note-taking is done before that great Victorian invention, the herbaceous border. Here, in a long strip against an old redbrick wall pockmarked by generations of support nails, plants are grown in descending order of height, with the tallest, the delphiniums, up against the wall-trained trees at the back. From November to March the bed has little to show but some damp, brown stumps. Then the glory of the English year begins. Month by month the border displays different plants of different hues like swelling movements in a symphony of colour, until, in August and September, it comes to a blazing finale of asters.

The colours of England, as exemplified in her gardens, are one of her unique features. The light itself is gentle and rich; clear sunshine gives everything the translucent splendour of a stained glass window; on more overcast days we can get the misty opacity of a Chinese painting. The beauty of all lands depends on the disposition of the elements, and the particular god who favours England is rain. We complain about it, but we complain more and with better cause when there is a drought. The rain which leadens the sky, wets our feet and floods our meadows, sometimes to such an extent that it is a wonder that we don't grow rice, is the rain that fills the streams, nourishes the gardens and makes a watercolour masterpiece of the landscape. Asked what he considered to be the thing most unique to England, a Cypriot diplomat responded without hesitation: 'The colour green.'

The landscape has been made by man. The conscious effort he has put into it, the care with which he has attended it, the devotion which he has bestowed upon it, reflect back on him a true image of himself and fill him with awe of the Divine. The benign face of Divinity which is the English countryside has been the inspiration of English artists. To list the names of the poets, painters and musicians who have been inspired by the manifest beauty of the land is itself a kind of music, a litany of Englishness: Shakespeare, Herbert, Donne, Wordsworth, Coleridge, Keats, Eliot, Thomas, Auden and Betjeman; Constable, Cotman, Girtin, Crome, Turner and Blake; Dunstable, Byrd, Tallis, Taverner, Purcell, Parry, Holst, Delius, Vaughan Williams, Walton, Elgar and Britten. These are only a few of the names of men who have been inspired by the English countryside and in their turn have inspired the country. Two areas have enjoyed particular veneration as a result: East Anglia, the home of the Norwich School of watercolour painters and Britten's Aldeburgh; and the west country of Gloucestershire, Herefordshire and Shropshire, which include the Malverns of Elgar and William Langland.

What such artists and their work have in common is a certain sound reflecting a certain quality: love. It is a dispassionate love, quiet, gentle and, at heart, ineffable.

Divinity is reflected in all creation, but whereas in some landscapes one meets the aspects of fear and awe, in England one meets the mystery. Gaze long enough and the scene begins to shimmer like gauze. In certain lights, particularly at dawn or dusk, or in spring and autumn, one may find oneself standing at the very threshold between one reality and another.

*The coast at
Morwenstow,
North Devon*

Let then the youth go back, as
occasion will permit, to nature
and to solitude. A world of fresh
sensations will gradually open
upon him, as, instead of being
propelled restlessly towards
others in admiration or too
hasty love, he makes it his prime
business to understand himself.

WILLIAM WORDSWORTH:
Reply to 'Mathetes'

THE LAW
IS ABOVE YOU

Reason is the life
of the law; nay,
the common law
itself is nothing
else but reason.

SIR EDWARD COKE:
The Institutes of
the Law of England

The judges' lodgings near Lincoln Cathedral, as seen from the castle ramparts

The statue of Alfred the Great overlooking the Broadway, Winchester

At the heart of the Common Law of England lie three assumptions: that man is essentially good, that all men are equal under the law, and that he who does not transgress the law is free. This is natural law but we have arrived at it with that mixture of inspiration and labour that Michelangelo took to find the ideal form within a block of marble. The marble god has stood in the halls of our history for some time now, long enough for it to be taken for granted by most, long enough for it to have become the butt of mockery for some, long enough for us no more to see and wonder at its beauty. Before it is sold off to a museum of fine antiquities, we should consider it again.

The story begins at a place we do not know, at a time we can only guess at, with the first Anglo-Saxons and their *dooms*. These *dooms*, or statutes, were passed on orally until the arrival of Christianity. With the new religion came writing and, with the monkish scribes came the Christianization of what was written. It is now difficult to find within these early medieval texts the original old Germanic laws and the most ancient of our customs. There is however a distinctive sound to English law which may well have been there from the beginning. Expressed in a word, it is freedom. Freedom is an ancient word rooted far back in the Sanskrit language and the Indo-European tradition. It signifies 'the law of friends', which is entirely appropriate to a system which, as Lord Denning once said, is based on love. With the arrival of Christianity, the Christian concept of love seems to have matched what the Anglo-Saxon considered to be reasonable. There are two passages from Christian scripture which most exemplify the English idea of justice, one from the Old Testament one from the New:

It is, I suggest to you, a most significant thing that a judge should draw his principles of law, or rather his principles of justice, from the Christian commandment of love. I do not know where else he is to find them. Some people speak of natural justice as though it was a thing well recognisable by anyone, whatever his training or upbringing. But I am quite sure that our conception of it is entirely due to our habits of thought through many generations. The common law of England has been moulded for centuries by judges who have been brought up in the Christian faith. The precepts of religion, consciously or unconsciously, have been their guide in the administration of justice.

LORD DENNING: Centennial Address to the Lawyer's Prayer Union, 1952

Thou shalt not avenge nor bear any grudge against the children of thy people, but thou shalt love thy neighbour as thyself: I am the Lord (Leviticus 19:18); and Therefore all things whatsoever ye would that men should do to you, do ye even so to them: for this is the law and the prophets (Matthew 7:12).

In his Book of Laws King Alfred set out those laws of his predecessors which he wished to see continued and blended with them the Ten Commandments and principles of the New Testament. To these ingredients he then added a touch of magic: he inverted the Golden Rule 'Do unto others as you would that they should do unto you' to state 'What ye will that other men shall not do to you, that do ye not to other men.' This became the ruling guide to true relations not only between neighbours but also between the judge and the plaintiff. The laws of Alfred, amplified by his successors, grew into a body of law called custom. Customary law is not common law, however, until one unified nation is abiding by one set of laws, and that is two hundred years hence in our story.

Meanwhile it is 1066. During this interruption to Anglo-Saxon history, we will take the opportunity to look abroad and see what other systems of law were in existence. In the centuries surrounding the lifetime of Christ, much of Europe was unified by one rule, that of the Roman Empire. The empire collapsed rather like a plant where the top has become too heavy for the roots. As the plant fell, it released the seeds of Christianity. The conversion of the Romans had begun with the slave classes and spread to the masters. By the fourth century AD the Romans were largely a Christianizing force but they were also a dying force. With society breaking down, civilized life became eclipsed by the demands of simple survival.

... the like natural inducement hath brought men to know that it is their duty no less to love others than themselves. For seeing those things which are equal must needs have all one measure; if I cannot but wish to receive all good, even as much at everyman's hand as any man can wish unto his own soul, how should I look to have any part of my desire herein satisfied, unless myself be careful to satisfy the like desire which is undoubtedly in other men, we all being of one and the same nature?

RICHARD HOOKER: Of the Laws of Ecclesiastical Polity

Digests and codes imposed in the Roman manner by an omnipotent state on a subject people were alien to the spirit and tradition of England. The law was already there, in the customs of the land, and it was only a matter of discovering it by diligent study and comparison of recorded decisions in earlier cases and applying it to the particular dispute before the court.

… the liberties of Englishmen rested not on any enactment of the State but on immemorial slow-growing custom declared by juries of free men who gave their verdicts case by case in open court.

WINSTON CHURCHILL: A History of the English-Speaking Peoples

This is the era known as the 'Dark Ages'. As any gardener knows in winter, however, darkness is the harbinger not of death but of life. It is creative; it is the natural condition for the growth of seeds. The outstanding quality of the seeds sown in these centuries was spiritual; in this bed grew the institutions and nations of Europe, the result of cross-fertilization between Imperial and Christian Rome.

The organization of the Church was, like the Empire before it, centred on Rome, with the place of the Emperor being taken by the Pope. The genius of ancient Rome had been in its codifying and legal structures and the Church, requiring a body of law under which to unify its disparate and far-flung members, turned to the Digest of the fourth-century emperor, Justinian. For centuries church (or canon) law and civil law were barely distinguishable. As England converted to Christianity so canon law began to jostle with the customary laws of the shires and hundreds.

We need to return to the Normans to find out how this conflict was resolved. Of the Norman Conquest, the great scholar and judge Sir William Blackstone wrote: 'The nation at this period seems to have groaned under as absolute a slavery as was in the power of a warlike, an ambitious, and a politic prince to create … The law, too, as well as the prayers, were administered in an unknown tongue. The ancient trial by jury gave way to the impious decision by battle. The forest laws totally restrained all rural pleasures and manly recreations. And in cities and towns the case was no better; all company being obliged to disperse, and fire and candle to be extinguished, by eight at night, at the sound of the melancholy curfew.' [*Book IV, Ch. 3 Commentaries*].

Hadrian's Wall,
Northumberland,
from Walltown Crags

But even William the Conqueror, not otherwise noted for Anglomania, was subject to those forces which shaped this nation, particularly in the realm of law. In creating separate courts both temporal and spiritual, he freed the cleric from layman's laws, and the layman from clerical laws. He also had to recognize something that English nature insists upon: that there is such a thing as a free man. The concept of the free man, and its corollary, the unfree man, was general in Europe and indeed had existed in Anglo-Saxon England. Under the Normans, however, there were degrees of slavery: the slave proper, the villein and the serf. Thus the numbers of the 'unfree' had increased considerably and to be bound became considered as 'normal'. Everyman was tied to a master. But what is normal is not always natural, and it was for the law – the working of nature in society – to set men free.

Duke William had brought with him to England an abbot called Lanfranc. Lanfranc was a master of law from Lombardy, where the first law schools of Christian Europe had been founded. Educated in these schools, he became well-versed in each of the various systems of law then current, seeking always the similarities between them in the hope of establishing harmony and unity. Believing that the just way to govern a subject nation is by means of its own laws and customs, when he arrived in England Lanfranc set about mastering the Anglo-Saxon *dooms*. Under Norman occupation the language of English law became French; that the spirit of the law remained English was largely due to Lanfranc. The same honour of native tradition was to be displayed centuries later when an English judge called Sir William Jones set himself to study Hindu laws to facilitate good governance of India. To govern well, one must have respect for custom. For a fine definition of what a custom is, here is that of Sir John Davies who, in his Irish Reports of 1674, wrote:

'When a reasonable act once done is found to be good and beneficial to the people, and agreeable to their nature and disposition, then do they use it and practise it again and again, and so by often iteration and multiplication of the act it becometh a custom; and being continued without interruption time out of mind, it obtaineth the force of a Law.

And this Customary Law is the most perfect and most excellent, and without comparison the best, to make and preserve a Commonwealth. For the written laws which are made ... by the Edicts of Princes ... are imposed upon the Subject before any trial or probation made, whether the same be fit and agreeable to the nature and disposition of the people, or whether they will breed any inconvenience or no. But a Custom doth never become a Law to bind the people, until it hath been tried and approved time out of mind ...'

Though the customs of England were recognized by Lanfranc, they were not revived until the following century when the king turned to them for the establishment of the Common Law. Henry II is popularly remembered as the estranged husband of Eleanor of Aquitaine, the tempestuous father of Richard and John, and the fiery opponent of Becket. Strange then that he, one of nature's more splenetic, argumentative sons, and a Frenchman at that, should be instrumental in the rebirth in England of freedom-under-law. Throughout his reign he made decisions that would turn the English desire for freedom from a nurtured ideal into

An Anglo-Saxon law stone, or seat of judgement, at Leighton Bromswold, Huntingdonshire

The nearest we can get to defining justice is to say that it is what the right-minded members of the community — those who have the right spirit within them — believe to be fair.

LORD DENNING: The Road to Justice

an attainable goal. The first such decision was to consult men wiser than himself. Some of their names are known to us, such as Pattishall, Rayleigh and Ranulf Glanville, but others go unrecorded. What seems evident, however, is that Henry's wisdom was inspired by men of the platonic tradition and the twelfth-century Renaissance.

Henry's genius lay not in devising new laws but in making certain innovations which were to affect the course of English law profoundly. One was to divide the country into circuits and to send out judges across the land to administer justice. This decision was recorded by a contemporary:

'The bishops, earls and magnates of the realm being assembled at Windsor [in the year 1179], the king by their common counsel ... divided England into four parts. For each part he appointed wise men from his kingdom and later sent them through the regions of the kingdom assigned to them to execute justice among the people ... Thus he took care to provide for men's needs by setting apart from the generality of mankind those who, albeit they live among men and watch over them, yet possess qualities of insight and boldness superior to those of an ordinary man.'

Another of Henry's innovations was a new use of the jury. In its original, Frankish, form a jury was a body of men summoned by the king to provide information on local rights and customs and thereby to settle administrative matters. Henry saw the potential in having a jury decide cases which for the generations since the Conquest had been decided by a judge alone, or even by battle. The first English juries were called to witness rather than to judge the facts. The development of the jury as an impartial instrument of judgement was a long one.

Codrington Library, All Souls, Oxford. Against much opposition from the architect Nicholas Hawksmoor, Blackstone held out for a large library to be built

Statue of Sir William Blackstone by John Bacon

It is one of the characteristic marks of English liberty, that our common law depends on custom; which carries this internal evidence of freedom along with it, that it probably was introduced by the voluntary consent of the people.

WILLIAM BLACKSTONE: Commentaries on the Laws of England

One of the many great principles of English law is that it is better that a guilty man should go unpunished than that an innocent man should suffer. The once-required unanimity of a jury was a powerful guarantee of this principle. However the use of juries has been reduced and is now largely confined to criminal trials. It is for us to safeguard with utmost care what still remains for, as Blackstone said, 'However convenient these [arbitrary powers of trial by justices of the peace, commissioners of the revenue, and courts of conscience] may appear at first ... yet let it be remembered, that delays, and little inconveniences in the forms of justice, are the price that all free nations must pay for their liberty in more substantial matters; that these inroads upon this sacred bulwark of the nation are fundamentally opposite to the spirit of our constitution; and that, though begun in trifles, the precedent may gradually increase and spread, to the utter disuse of juries in questions of the most momentous concern.'

The reign of Henry II saw the initiation of the rule of law and yet, for all the significance of that great work, it was still rudimentary. The sculptor had merely outlined the form he could see within the block of marble. It was for later men to chisel the stone and free the form. And here the analogy with sculpture breaks down, for law is not a frozen form but a living one. Step by step through the centuries it has, with the help of its servants, freed itself from faults and accretions. Henry II had left it with one fault so deforming that the law itself acted within a generation. That fault was Henry's presumption, based on that of his father and of his father's father before him, that the King was above the law.

The reign of King John proved the opposite to be true. John so vaunted

Runnymede by the Thames, Surrey

himself above the law, was so impervious to all that was reasonable, that the lawful result was the confrontation with a group of barons on a watermeadow near Windsor Castle. At Runnymede the King abjectly signed the charter that would check once and for all such an abuse of power. In Churchill's inimitable words: 'The leaders of the barons in 1215 groped in the dim light towards a fundamental principle. Government must henceforward mean something more than the arbitrary rule of any man, and custom and the law must stand even above the King. It was this idea, perhaps only half understood, that gave unity and force to the barons' opposition and made the Charter … imperishable.'

Law has a way of asserting itself despite the nature of the men wielding it. The barons who forced John to sign the Magna Carta had not drawn up the charter with English liberty in mind; they merely called upon the concept to achieve their own ends. The Magna Carta lists specific remedies for specific evils and does not read as a list of principles. In the sum of it, however, lies freedom. King John, who had been so iniquitous as to pawn the nation to the Pope, had to be checked: the law used the barons, not the barons the law.

Among the bravest men in English history are those who stand fearlessly for what they believe to be right. Stephen Langton, Archbishop of Canterbury and first signatory of the Great Charter, stood up to both monarch and Pope, and championed the cause of English rights into the reign of Henry III. It was during that reign that a Judge of Assize, Henry of Bracton, wrote *A Tract on the Laws and Customs of England*. Bracton has since been called the Father of the Common Law. His work was the foundation for the English system, since adopted in many parts of

The jury system has come to stand for all we mean by English justice, because so long as a case has to be scrutinised by twelve honest men defendant and plaintiff alike have a safeguard from arbitrary perversion of the law. It is this which distinguishes the law administered in English courts from Continental legal systems based on Roman law. Thus amidst the great process of centralisation [during the reign of Henry II] the old principle was preserved, and endures to this day, that law flows from the people, and is not given by the King.

WINSTON CHURCHILL: A History of the English-Speaking Peoples

A free man is his own man; one who is master of his own acts and answerable for them, one who lives on his own, who is able to manage and maintain his own family and rear and educate his own children; one who is able to administer his own property and his own affairs, in a society which is conceived as an association of families of free and lawful men and women, living in the fellowship of a free community.

RICHARD O'SULLIVAN: The Inheritance of the Common Law

The very idea of a normal person is the creation of a common law which has strengthened the bonds of Society by admitting an equal justice to all its members.

SIR WILLIAM HOLDSWORTH
(quoted by O'Sullivan)

the world, in which the Common Law is commented upon rather than defined, leaving it open to further development and expansion. In his work, Bracton made a resounding statement about the law's supremacy: 'The king has no equal within his realm. Subjects cannot be the equals of the ruler, because he would thereby lose his rule, since equal can have no authority over equal: not *a fortiori* a superior, because he would then be subject to those subjected to him. The king must not be under man but under God and the law, because law makes the king. Let him therefore bestow upon the law what the law bestows on him, namely, rule and power: for there is no king where will rules rather than law.' This truth has been restated several times since, and always at great risk to the speaker. Chief Justice Fortescue, as tutor to the future Edward IV, instructed the prince of the king's place under law. And in response to the Stuart misconception about the divine right of kings, Chief Justice Coke challenged James I with the same principle. Now, thanks to Thomas Fuller and, more recently, Lord Denning, 'Be you never so high, the law is above you', has become the great sentence of restraint upon arrogance and the abuse of power.

Of the new spirit that had entered Europe in the Dark Ages perhaps its sweetest principle was that all men are equal in the eye of the Lord. Christianity, which had been preached to the Roman masters by their slaves, did not tolerate the idea of the ownership of one man by another. Slavery had been common in the pre-Christian world but, with the coming of the new religion, it began to decline in Europe, at least in the form of one Christian being enslaved by another. In the sixth century Pope Gregory found some young men for sale in the slave market of Rome.

*Wildy and Sons,
established in 1830,
booksellers to the
Inns of Court,
London*

Impressed by them, he made enquiries and, told that they were Angles, thought there had been some mistake. 'Not angles,' said the Pope, 'but angels.' The incident inspired the mission of St Augustine and, in turning the English into Christians, Gregory and Augustine freed them henceforward from slavery. The trade in enslaved heathens was a different matter. That flourished. The magnificent work of the Quaker William Wilberforce, which led to the abolition of the British slave trade in 1833, could not have taken place but for the efforts made in previous centuries in the realm of the law.

Although slavery as such had become extinct in England by the end of the twelfth century, the villein or bonded labourer still existed; indeed, medieval society depended upon him and his work. His cause was advanced by the Constitutions of Clarendon (1164), in which the concept of the free and lawful man was introduced. It was set back again by an academic move to tidy up the administration, which resulted in equating the status of the villein with that of the *servus* of Roman civil law. This deprived the villein of his property for centuries. The wrong was redressed quietly, within the workings of the law itself, but it was not until the fifteenth century that the villein was at last emancipated. So slow and imperceptible was the change that no trumpets blew to herald the moment, but change there was and the villein became the 'copyholder'. Sir Edward Coke, in the *Complete Copyholder*, noted that: 'copyholders stand upon a sure ground, now they weigh not their Lord's displeasure, they shake not at every sudden blast of wind! they eat, drink and sleep securely only having a special care of the main Chance, viz.: to perform carefully what Duties and Services soever their Tenure doth exact

Methinketh it first good to see whether it may stand with conscience that one may claim another to be his villein and that he may take from him his land and goods, and put his body in prison if he will: it seemeth hee loveth not his neighbour as himself that doth so to him.

CHRISTOPHER ST. GERMAN:
Doctor and Student

and Custom doth require: then let the Lord frown, the Copyholder cares not knowing himself safe and not within any danger.'

As Richard O'Sullivan said in *The Inheritance of the Common Law*, 'The transformation over a whole course of centuries of slave and serf and villein into the copyholder and the yeoman is a singular proof of the power and the energy of a great ideal.' The work did not stop there. Apart from having to maintain such rights and freedoms, which is work requiring constant vigilance, there was the further task of freeing those whose lot was far worse than that of the villeins: the slaves. For centuries the English prided themselves on having no slave trade within England, and the cargoes at the ports showed no sign of a slave trade outside the country. But all was not as it seemed. The English goods exported to Africa were exchanged for black Africans, who were then shipped to America to be bartered for American goods. Thus while from ports like Bristol goods of British manufacture went out and American plantation products, such as sugar, rum, cotton and coffee, came in, the human deprivation and misery involved in the exchange was hidden from public view. Self-deception is something which cannot survive the light of reason. With a judge such as Lord Mansfield speaking the truth, the law prepared the ground for Wilberforce.

The speech of a judge can be as important, if not more important, than the decisions of a judge. It can certainly be as effective and influential. All it requires is fearlessness. And independence.

When the differences between ecclesiastical and civil laws were established, the priests withdrew from the Bench and left the business of civil law to lay lawyers.

Fountain's Court,
Middle Temple, London

Of equal intellectual vigour, the lay lawyers had the additional advantage of worldly knowledge and the experience of being husbands and fathers, unlike the clerics who were educated in the scholastic arena of the universities. According to Maitland, 'They are in their way learned, cultivated men, linguists, logicians, tenacious disputants, true lovers of the nice case and the moot point. They are gregarious, clubable men, grouping themselves in hospices which became schools of law, multiplying manuscripts, arguing, learning and teaching, the great mediators between life and logic, a reasoning, reasonable element in the English nation.' These clubs or associations of lawyers became housed at the Inns of Court, of which there are four: Middle Temple, Inner Temple, Lincoln's Inn and Gray's Inn. Together they constitute a university of law, a hidden university without the fame and glamour of Oxbridge, but a university which has been attended by some of the finest minds in English history. As O'Sullivan put it, 'Throughout the whole period of its creative life and power the Common Law of England was in touch with, sensitive to, and nourished by the tradition of classical and Christian philosophy and theology. Fortified and inspired by all this learning, and their own constant ideals, the Masters and Apprentices at law of the Inns of Court – lawyers and judges like Herle and Gascoigne, Fortescue and Littleton, Rede and St. German, and Thomas More and Edmund Plowden – elaborated over a series of centuries a body of law – private law and public law, for the English constitution is part of the Common Law – that illustrated and embodied the great conceptions of the dignity and the freedom and responsibility of Everyman that were from the beginning a distinguishing feature of the Common Law of England.'

The Common Law starts with man as he is, with man in his actual constitution, as a reasonable being: the reasonable man of the law. Man thus considered is a being of spirit and of sense.

RICHARD O'SULLIVAN: The Inheritance of the Common Law

The figure of Justice on the top of the Criminal Courts of Justice, the Old Bailey, London

The freedom of the individual, which is so dear to us, has to be balanced with his duty; for to be sure every one owes a duty to the society of which he forms part. The balance has changed remarkably during the last 100 years. Previously the freedom of the individual carried with it a freedom to acquire and use his property as he wished, a freedom to contract and so forth: but these freedoms were so much abused that in our time they have been counter-balanced by the duty to use one's property and powers for the good of society as a whole. In some foreign countries this duty has been carried to such a pitch that freedom, as we know it, no longer exists. If the people of those countries choose to put up with such a system that is their affair. All that needs to be said about it is that it is not the English view of human society. What matters in England is that each man should be free to develop his own personality to the full: and the only duties which should restrict this freedom are those which are necessary to enable everyone else to do the same.

LORD DENNING: Freedom Under the Law

Laws of Reason have these marks to be known by. Such as keep them resemble most lively in their voluntary actions that very manner of working which Nature herself doth necessarily observe in the course of the whole world. The works of Nature are all behoveful, beautiful, without superfluity or defect; even so theirs, if they be framed according to that which the Law of Reason teacheth.

RICHARD HOOKER: Of the Laws of Ecclesiastical Polity

Everyman is presumed at Common Law to be a good and lawful man, although subject of course to human frailty. As Erasmus said, 'Nature, or rather God, hath shaped this creature (that is, Man) not to war but to friendship, not to destruction but to health, not to wrong but to kindness and benevolence'. In the sixteenth century there arose two schools of thought as to the nature of Man. One, following Erasmus and Richard Hooker, saw that nature as being essentially good; the other, typified by Thomas Hobbes, considered that the life of man is nasty, brutish and short. English law agrees with Hooker and, even today, it is this naturally good, kind man who, if he stands accused of being otherwise, remains innocent in the light of the law until the burden of proof tips the scales of justice against him. Hobbes's man is the creation of corrupt, totalitarian systems, but the concept of the free man, as liable to duties as he is to rights, is the creation of the English Common Law.

Following the removal of James II by Parliament, and his replacement by William and Mary in the 'Glorious Revolution' of 1688, came the new constitutional arrangement embodied in the Bill of Rights. In assuring the ascendancy of parliamentary power over sovereign rights, however, the Bill placed Parliament in the seat just vacated by the king, that of being above the law. In the twentieth century the consequences of that are being felt in increasing strength. Here is what the Scottish judge Lord Macmillan had to say about it in 1950: 'The lover of our ancient laws and institutions … cannot but look with some dismay at

In societies where constitutional rights are assured, co-operation between all citizens becomes more natural and more fruitful in tackling the major problems we face. The achievement of one human value can help to achieve others. We should all aspire to raise the standards of life in our countries, to achieve a more prosperous and equitable society and to exercise a powerful influence for peace within and between nations.

None of this is easy to bring about because the establishment of human values implies duties as well as rights. If we want to exercise and enlarge our rights and opportunities, we have to safeguard the rights and opportunities of others. We should look for chances to give service just as eagerly as we look for benefits for ourselves.

HER MAJESTY QUEEN ELIZABETH II:
Commonwealth Day Message, 1993

the process which we see daily in operation around us, whereby the customary Common Law of the land, which has served us so well in the past, is being more and more superseded by a system of laws which have no regard for the usages and customs of the people, but are dictated by 'ideological theories'. There will soon be little of the Common Law left either in England or in Scotland, and the Statute Book and vast volumes of statutory rules and orders will take its place.'

Statute law, the laws of temporary expediency, are the province of Parliament. Their mushrooming comes from an idea: that to rule requires winning the majority of votes. Therefore government does what the electorate likes. Individually we all know how hard it is to choose the good over the pleasant. How much harder it is then for government to enact the good rather than that which pleases the majority and wins the votes.

As Edmund Burke said in a speech on the Acts of Uniformity in 1772, '… all who administer in the government of men, in which they stand in the person of God Himself, should have high and worthy notions of their function and destination; that their hope should be full of immortality; that they should not look to the paltry pelf of the moment, nor to the temporary and transient praise of the vulgar, but to a solid, permanent existence, in the permanent part of their nature, and to a permanent fame and glory, in the example they leave as a rich inheritance to the world.'

In entering the world of Parliament, we have entered that of the English constitution. Meaning literally 'to stand together', the constitution is the foundation of a nation; in England it is a creation of the common law. It is a subtle thing,

The spirit of truth and justice is not something you can see. It is not temporal but eternal.

LORD DENNING: broadcast on BBC Home Service, 14 September 1943

represented by various institutions such as monarchy, government, church, university and courts of law, which together but in their different ways, speak and act in accordance with those principles which the nation holds dear. The Magna Carta, the Petition of Right and the Bill of Rights embody some of those principles, such as the right of a man not to be imprisoned 'without just cause or due process of law'; they do not, however, form a written constitution. A written constitution is a human document. An unwritten constitution is a recognition that law is above man and that its workings depend on reason. Even today one may sense the spirit of Magna Carta still working in the development of the nation, and in a manner which a fixed constitution would prevent.

There is no doubt that to most people, including the English themselves, the English constitution is a puzzle and a mystery. We see it in the colourful trappings of state events, but few people truly understand its workings. They would be even fewer without Walter Bagehot and his beautiful book *The English Constitution*. Bagehot, a Victorian banker who became a journalist and editor of *The Economist*, enjoyed a clarity and simplicity of understanding which he could convey in blunt, straightforward prose. Gladstone called him his 'spare Chancellor'. To read *The English Constitution* is often to receive the disconcerting sensation of being like a puppet who is suddenly shown the strings and how they are pulled.

At the centre of the constitution stands the monarchy. Royalty is a concept common to all mankind, though its forms are various. Early English royalty was elective, the king being chosen from amongst the chiefs, each of whom claimed descent from the god Woden. Therefore from the very beginning monarchy and

The quality of mercy is not strain'd;
It droppeth as the gentle rain from heaven
Upon the place beneath. It is twice blest:
It blesseth him that gives and him that takes.
'Tis mightiest in the mightiest; it becomes
The throned monarch better than his crown;
His sceptre shows the force of temporal power,
The attribute to awe and majesty,
Wherein doth sit the dread and fear of kings;
But mercy is above this sceptred sway,
It is enthroned in the hearts of kings,
It is an attribute of God himself;
And earthly power doth then show likest God's
When mercy seasons justice.

SHAKESPEARE: THE Merchant of Venice

divinity were related in the minds of men, with the king seen as the mediator between heaven and earth and the agent of the justice of God.

The first place of coronation in Anglo-Saxon England was Winchester but in the time of Edward the Confessor the honour was transferred to Westminster Abbey. Everything with which the monarch is invested during coronation is symbolic: the Swords of Justice and Mercy, the Orb signifying the world subject to the power of Christ; the ring of kingly dignity; and the two Sceptres, one with the cross of power and justice, the other with a dove symbolizing equity and mercy. But the heart of the ceremony is the consecration of the monarch. This element of the service was added in the tenth century by St Dunstan, Archbishop of Canterbury, who revised the whole rite of coronation. Dunstan elevated the act into a solemn ceremony, making its most sacred moment not the crowning but the anointing, a rite drawn from the consecration of priests. Such is the significance of this moment that it was not televised during the coronation of Queen Elizabeth II. Dunstan's long career, in which he revived monasticism and the Rule of St Benedict in England, began in the court of King Alfred's grandson, Athelstan, who was the first king to rule all England. With Athelstan came majesty to the monarchy: such was his splendid reputation throughout western Europe that he was invested with some of the regalia of Charlemagne. But at the very time when kingship came to mean power and gorgeousness, there was the ascetic monk in the form of Dunstan, standing as a reminder that power is a divine gift and sacred trust.

English kings have rarely been perfect. 'Our country has produced millions of blameless greengrocers but not one blameless monarch,' says King Magnus in

The Sovereign's Sceptre with Cross, and the Sovereign's Sceptre with Dove

Of all odd forms of government, the oddest really is government by a public meeting. Here are 658 persons, collected from all parts of England, different in nature, different in interest, different in look, and language. If we think what an empire the English is, how various are its components, how incessant its concerns, how immersed in history its policy; if we think what a vast information, what a nice discretion, what a consistent will ought to mark the rulers of that empire, – we shall be surprised when we see them ... You have not a perception of the first elements in this matter till you know that government by a club is a standing wonder.

WALTER BAGEHOT: The English Constitution

As long as you have the wisdom to keep the sovereign authority of this country as the sanctuary of liberty, the sacred temple consecrated to our common faith, wherever the chosen race and sons of England worship freedom, they will turn their faces towards you. The more they multiply, the more friends you will have; the more ardently they love liberty, the more perfect will be their obedience. Slavery they can have anywhere. It is a weed that grows in every soil ... But, until you become lost to all feeling of your true interest and your natural dignity, freedom they can have from none but you.

EDMUND BURKE: address to the House of Commons on Conciliation with America, 1775

Shaw's *The Apple Cart*. Often someone has to step in to restrain their excesses, whether it be an Archbishop, the barons or, more recently, parliamentary representatives of the people. But the English genius has been to retain a constitutional monarchy at the heart of its government. Walter Bagehot explains:

'The best reason why Monarchy is a strong government is, that it is an intelligible government. The mass of mankind understand it, and they hardly anywhere in the world understand any other. It is often said that men are ruled by their imaginations; but it would be truer to say they are governed by the weakness of their imaginations. The nature of a constitution, the action of an assembly, the play of parties, the unseen formation of a guiding opinion, are complex facts, difficult to know and easy to mistake. But the action of a single will, the fiat of a single mind, are easy ideas: anybody can make them out, and no one can ever forget them.'

Put simply, one is better than many. Over the years the role of the monarch has been refined until the direct powers have been assumed by Parliament, and yet the monarch's powers of influence remain immense. But the stature of the monarchy fluctuates. During the reign of the Hanoverians it reached such a low level that the last of them was vilified in his obituary in *The Times*. It was Queen Victoria who regained the monarchy's place in the nation's heart. That love felt by the nation has been rewarded by the quality of the kings and queens of the twentieth century. Through the particular work of George V and George VI, the monarchy has come to represent a benign power of unity which, from a removed distance, safeguards the nation. It was a wise decision when, during the first war

Houses of Parliament from
the Thames Embankment

with Germany, George V chose to disengage his family from their European relations. What is in a name? Much. Overnight the house of Saxe-Coburg-Gotha became the House of Windsor, and the English monarchy entered an unprecedented phase of popularity. Since then, and particularly in the person of Elizabeth II, the monarchy has devoted itself with dignity and restraint to the service of the nation. The sovereignty of a nation rests in its monarch, and may be defined as 'the ultimate power in the state to let right be done'. In the monarchy lies the stability of the nation; we abolish it at our peril. Nations that copy English parliamentary democracy in the hope of obtaining good government would do well to remember that it is the King-in-Parliament which gives an underlying unity to the three branches of government: executive, legislative and judiciary. That unity is the real strength of English government.

In fact, the best form of government is self-government. In England the common law and the constitution are founded on principles of personal responsibility and duty. But wherever people abrogate responsibility for their own actions, states have to assume greater powers of control. The aim of parliamentary democracy controlling a constitutional monarchy is to prevent that assumption of power becoming excessive.

Parliament consists of the Queen, the House of Lords and the House of Commons. It has not always been so. Once it was just the lords, those men of high office who formed the council of the king which, in Anglo-Saxon times, was called the *witan*. Over the centuries government and constitution have evolved slowly, often imperceptibly, reflecting changes in the nation and the national mood (so

The House of Lords, as a House, is not a bulwark that will keep out revolution, but an index that revolution is unlikely.

WALTER BAGEHOT:
The English Constitution

The principle of Parliament is obedience to leaders. Change your leader if you will, take another if you will, but obey No. 1 while you serve No. 1, and obey No. 2 when you have gone over to No. 2. The penalty of not doing so is the penalty of impotence. It is not that you will not be able to do any good, but you will not be able to do anything at all. If everybody does what he thinks right, there will be 657 amendments to every motion, and none of them will be carried or the motion either.

WALTER BAGEHOT:
The English Constitution

It may seem odd to say so, just after inculcating that party organisation is the vital principle of representative government, but that organization is permanently efficient, because it is not composed of warm partisans. The body is eager, but the atoms are cool. If it were otherwise, parliamentary government would become the worst of governments – a sectarian government. The party in power would go all the lengths their orators proposed – all that their formulae enjoined, as far as they had ever said they would go. But the partisans of the English Parliament are not of such a temper. They are Whigs, or Radicals, or Tories, but they are much else too. They are common Englishmen, and, as Father Newman complains, 'hard to be worked up to the dogmatic level'. They are not eager to press the tenets of their party to impossible conclusions. On the contrary, the way to lead them – the best and acknowledged way – is to affect a studied and illogical moderation.

WALTER BAGEHOT: The English Constitution

imperceptibly that for instance, no-one knows the precise date of the inception of the Cabinet). These days the part played in the proceedings of Parliament, both by the monarch and the lords, is limited, almost ritualized, and the daily business of government is done by the prime minister, the Cabinet, and ministers appointed from elected members of Parliament in the House of Commons. But laws may not be ratified without royal assent, acts may not be passed without the support of the House of Lords, and generally the government cannot act without the support of a majority of all elected members of Parliament.

Until about a hundred and fifty years ago, most members of Parliament were drawn from the great families of the aristocracy and landowning classes. The various Reform Acts in 1832, 1867 and 1884 led to the redistribution of parliamentary seats and the extension of voting rights. Universal male suffrage, that is, 'one man one vote', preceded female suffrage by only a short period. About the same time, the Civil Service was undergoing the Northcote-Trevelyan reforms by which the first principle of selection became merit through fair and open competition. The service, which gives continuity to the process of government, demands of its officers nothing less than wholehearted integrity, impartiality, loyalty, discretion and honesty. As one civil servant put it, 'One is expected to give fearless advice to Ministers on the value and implications of possible courses of action, and then carry out the Minister's decision to the best of one's ability, even if one does not agree with it'.

All changes in government follow from changes in the nation, economic and social. The long, fascinating history of English government is the story of a living organism growing and developing from ancient times into the modern age. In the

days of Whig and Tory, it must have seemed to the people of England that there could only ever be Whigs and Tories. They were wrong, and so are we if it is presumed that there can only ever be Conservative and Labour, or even that there can only be two main contending parties. Government is as subject to change as any other living being. The day-to-day, mundane affairs of Parliament sometimes include decisions which, in years or generations to come, may result in unforseen changes to the constitution.

Despite the long history of English government, some things remain constant. One is that most ancient conception which has survived all foreign influence, even the Norman Conquest, namely that the government should consist of the King, the Council, and the people acting together, with the King's Peace over all. From this principle derives the doctrine that public affairs are settled by the joint agreement of the King-in-Parliament.

Another constant is that government is enacted by speech. That this is so is embodied in the very etymology of the word *parliament*, from the French *parler*, to speak, attached to the suffix *-ment*. This suffix, deriving from the Latin for *mind*, has come to mean 'the action of'. The Palace of Westminster has heard some truly great speeches; speeches to rouse the nation; speeches to arouse compassion; speeches to remind us of our duty to others. Parliament has four main purposes: redress of grievances, control of national finances, control of the executive, and legislation. Everything that is laid before it must be laid in the form of a question to which, after debate, the answer is Aye or No. The Anglo-Saxon love of rhythm, combined with the techniques of classical oratory learned during the Renaissance, have meant

… and every child that is born alive, is either a little Liberal or a little Conservative.

GILBERT AND SULLIVAN: Iolanthe

The lyrical function of
Parliament, if I may use such
a phrase, is well done; it
pours out in characteristic
words the characteristic
heart of the nation, and it
can do little more useful.

WALTER BAGEHOT: The English
Constitution

that, when we have been wise enough to choose a representative gifted with the power of speech, we have gained one with the power to rule. One has only to review the names of great British statesmen such as Pitt, Gladstone, Macaulay, Disraeli, Rosebery and Churchill to see that their fame rests not on what they did, what they thought, or what they believed, but on what they said.

The most effective speakers learnt their art in the debating societies of England's two great universities, Oxford and Cambridge. These two institutions, like so much else that is great and good in England, grew up naturally and were never formally instigated. In several cathedral cities or large market towns in medieval England, clerks licensed to teach attracted groups of young scholars. They lectured in churches or hired halls, lived in rented rooms, were vastly outnumbered by the townspeople and, like them, were under the rule of the sheriff.

Legend has it that Oxford University was founded by Alfred the Great. That is simply legend, but it may hold a clue to Oxford's beginnings. When Alfred wished to revive learning in Wessex, he turned to the kingdom of Mercia, where he found four suitable scholars. The rest of his advisers came from outside England. Oxford, then little more than a village, lay on the borderlands of Mercia and Wessex. It is not too fanciful to suppose that it was with Alfred's revival of learning that Oxford became a meeting place for scholars. Just as market towns grew up at crossroads where merchants met, perhaps at least one university grew up at a ford on the Thames where scholars met. Whatever the truth of Oxford's origins, its rise

above, say, Salisbury, Exeter or Lincoln, was due to the quality of its teachers during the thirteenth century when men such as England's Aristotle, Friar Roger Bacon, took the University to astounding heights of intellectual work.

The institutionalization of the University began with Walter de Merton, Bishop of Rochester, making funds available for the building of a college at Oxford. A few years later Peterhouse at Cambridge was built by the Bishop of Ely. According to Sir Maurice Powicke, 'They could not have had any idea that they were setting in motion a movement as strange as any of the strange things which our insular genius has turned into second nature'. There were earlier universities in Europe: Bologna, Padua and, contemporaneously, the Sorbonne, but only England could conceive of a university which was more of an idea than a place. Today our poor visitors wander perplexed in Oxford and Cambridge looking for 'the University'; they find colleges, but they find neither heart nor centre to the place. They demand of the natives, 'Where is the University?' but the natives do not know. The University, personified by its fellows and housed by its colleges, exists nowhere in the material world.

The relation of university to constitution is simple: it is the breeding ground of tomorrow's statesmen. Most if not all of our great orators have been born of the debating halls of university, public school or Inns of Court. But not all students are interested in public careers. Many spend their years at university devoting themselves to increasingly minute areas of specialization. With great intensity theses are written on such subjects as 'the effect of a cereal-based diet upon the civilization of Mesopotamia'. Perhaps as graduates they will never be called upon to

Our universities began not as institutions but as adventures of the mind.

73

think about such things again but they will have emerged from university with minds trained and ready to meet the practical problems of everyday life.

Most important of all will be the ideas they have formed at university, because these will give birth to the public opinion of the future. The ideas which dominate our thinking today were first being discussed in our universities twenty-five years ago. To know the future, discover the current ideas of students. In a generation they will govern society.

The constitution, embracing law, monarchy, government, church and university, is a subtle and flexible thing. Its real essence lies in the heart of man, in those intangible, magnificent qualities such as truth, freedom and justice, which are divine in origin.

No man is an Island, entire of itself; every man is a piece of the Continent, a part of the main; if a clod be washed away by the sea, Europe is the less, as well as if a promontory were, as well as if a manor of thy friends or of thine own were; any man's death diminishes me, because I am involved in Mankind; And therefore never send to know for whom the bell tolls; it tolls for thee.

JOHN DONNE: Devotions upon Emergent Occasions

75

ENGLISH

THE NATION'S TREASURE

Stand for truth;

it's enough.

BEN JONSON

One of the distinctive elements of Anglo-Saxon art was the knot. It is not always apparent but, behind the serpentine coils, twisting plaits and random tendrils, there was a geometric construction of squares, triangles and circles. The geometry of the knot was its foundation and was invisible in the finished work. Although it originated long before Christian theology, the knot design was based on the geometrical relationship of one and three. Geometry was the hidden secret of a good knot's ability to please. The unifying element of all those tendrils is in the underlying, invisible structure. It is the same with the English language.

Its history is one of turns and twists and change, with some changes so dramatic that the language is now divided into sections like a carpet page in the Lindisfarne Gospels. First there was Anglo-Saxon, or Old English, which was Germanic and an inflected language like Latin, Greek and Sanskrit. Then there was Middle English where the inflections were greatly reduced, the spelling was volatile, and the vocabulary borrowed much from French. The language called Modern English arose between 1450 and 1700. It has a grammar reduced to bare essentials, consistent – if illogical – spelling, and a vocabulary larger than that of any other language in the world.

The English language is a mongrel, with such a history of alteration, innovation and reformation that it seems improbable that anything we have today has any true equivalent in the past; that even in our enthusiastic celebration of 'heritage' we are identifying with people with whom we have little in common. Yet the human body can change dramatically in a lifetime without altering its identity;

Sound is eternal. If people truly understood that, they would be more careful what they composed and said.

Sir Thomas Beecham

from first teeth to false teeth, John Smith is still John Smith. Why that should be plunges us into philosophy, but suffice to say that the simple conclusion to this conundrum is that John Smith is not the name of a physical body only. Does the same apply to language?

The question is, if you speak a different language, are you of the same nation? Is it possible that, say, Alfred the Great, Chaucer and Shakespeare had each equal cause and claim to consider himself English? Were they able to meet beyond the constraints of space-time, what would these speakers of three tongues find in common?

Chaucer would probably comprehend most of the words of Alfred, but, confounded by the linguistic inventiveness of Shakespeare, might consider him a clever young upstart who makes free with the rules. Shakespeare in turn would be irritated by Chaucer's French terms, particularly his pronunciation of them, but would understand him well enough, whereas he might consider Alfred to be as foreign as the prince of Denmark. Poor Alfred would be listening to two foreigners who had invented queer polyglot languages based on his own dear tongue. His understanding of them would rest entirely on the strength of his own French and Latin.

Over the ages, while the grammar has simplified beyond Alfred's recognition, the vocabulary has increased by a multitude of words either created from the native stock or drawn from other languages. Certain things, however, have remained the same. First, the core language itself, without which we could not speak English. Although they may be spelt or pronounced differently, thousands of native nouns

and verbs are still in use and, as we will see, anyone who wishes to speak effectively will resort to them. One of them is particularly worthy of attention. *Truth* is a word as thoroughly Anglo-Saxon as any we might find still extant. Its spelling has changed a little with time, but its meaning remains the same. *The Oxford English Dictionary* offers several words to describe it: fidelity, loyalty, steadfast allegiance. Apart from *steadfast*, each of these words has a Latin-French origin, and is a near synonym but not a true one. To approach its real meaning, we need to trace it back to the Indo-European and Sanskrit root *dru* which means 'wood'. The word *tree* has the same root. Our ancient forefathers, to describe this subtle thing, used the tree as a metaphor. No wonder, then, that the Anglo-Saxons revered the tree; like truth it is something ancient and yet alive, something firm but not unyielding, something majestic but not remote. The oak by which the first councils met was the very embodiment of their guiding principle. A good ruler will be interested in truth on any level but a tyrant is only told what he wants to hear. Under a dictatorship or any kind of rule which encourages sycophancy, truth is an exile. *The Oxford English Dictionary* which, as will be explained later, does not prescribe but, like the law, rests on precedent and custom, cites the first usage of the word to King Alfred. That of course was its first written usage. If our three heroes were discussing truth and wisdom, which is very likely, then Alfred would have understood much of what the others had to say. Both words were in the speech from the beginning, and it is the love of truth which has kept England free.

The word *free* is akin to *truth* in its ancient pedigree but, like *wisdom*, it has a chapter to itself in this book, for each of these words is fundamental to the three elements that form a nation: language, law and religion. With such concepts as truth and freedom at its heart, the English language has formed the English nation as much as it has been formed by it. Despite the changes forced upon the language by history it has retained its dearest words and, to a large extent, its rhythm.

The rhythm of English conforms to this day to the unique Germanic pattern, which is to put the stress on the root syllable of a word. Thus in a word such as *unforeseeable* we are talking essentially about sight, no matter what prefixes and suffixes have attached themselves to the word to bend its meaning. The Danish linguist, Otto Jespersen, one of the greatest authorities on English, considered this system of value-stressing to be 'an exact correspondence between the inner and outer world' and indicative of all the blunt-speaking Germanic peoples (English, Scandinavian and German).

Apart from rhythm and stress, our three authors might recognise other things in each other: a terseness of style, a tendency towards understatement, and a preference for monosyllables. Although the last has only appeared in time, the desire for it must have been there at the beginning for it to appear at all. Perhaps it was this desire for economy of speech which has led to the national fondness for abbreviation (e.g. ta, hi, bye-bye, TV, OTT, etc.). Above all, they would recognise in each other a natural leaning towards the poetic, and this not because each was a poet but because each was English.

The poetry of English, being so distinct from latinate poetry, goes largely unrecognized, but it is at the heart of English speech. Latin poetry, which has tended to set all the rules, is measured in 'feet' and has the sound of running,

Capital at the University Museum, Oxford, inspired by John Ruskin

Flee from the throng and
  dwell with truthfulness;
Let thy wealth suffice though
  it be small,
For hoard hath hate and
  climbing slipperyness,
The crowd hath envy and
  success blinds wholly;
Relish no more than shall
  keep thee strong.
Act well thyself, who can
  counsel others;
And truth shall deliver
  thee, have no dread.

CHAUCER: Truth, The Ballad
of Good Counsel

walking, marching or dancing. Old English poetry is marked by the half-line break and has the sound of the rise and fall of a wave, or of the oar pulling. The same marine sound can still be heard in English today, with words and sentences ending quietly like the sea sighing on the beach. Poetry with a strong, repetitive rhythm and an end-rhyme encourages hurry, but the measure of Old English poetry is steady and contemplative. It is alliterative and, in both its rhythm and alliteration, democratic: everyone could participate in it, and we still do. Common phrases like 'as bold as brass', 'as cool as a cucumber', 'from top to toe' have been formed on principles followed by the Anglo-Saxon bards. Similarly, things that go together in couples are named in a rhythmic formation of heavy-light stress: 'cup and saucer', 'bread and butter', 'free and easy'. This measure is called the *trochee*, and is a familiar sound in English (listen, for instance, to the sound of the names of the days of the week), but the measure which is widely thought to be most natural to the English language, and the one most used in poetry, is the *iamb*, which follows the pattern of light-heavy stress. The reason for this is the little words, often overlooked and disregarded, that English so depends upon. It is their presence in sentences that make the iambic measure natural to English speech. Thus a common phrase like 'as bold as brass' is not only alliterative but is also iambic in rhythm.

Now that our three heroes have recognised in each other something which we might call the same emotive force, we will leave them unified, if only in the desire to go down to the pub, while we re-enter the world of change or, as Chaucer might have called it, mutability.

Language is made up of many elements, of which the primary ones are grammar, vocabulary, pronunciation and spelling, and English has changed in each of these areas. Old English, being a grandchild of the first language of the Indo-Europeans, was an inflected language. That is to say that the place a word took in a sentence was indicated by the endings of nouns and verbs. It was the desire, or need, for simplification that caused most of the inflections to wither and die. Each kingdom of England had its own dialect, and the coming together of these into a national language would have affected grammar. The arrival of the Vikings brought linguistic changes, most significantly in the vocabulary, but it was the coming of the Normans which affected the language most profoundly and marked the break between Old and Middle English. Many inflections were lost and, to do their work, a host of unassuming little words called prepositions were brought into service. Suddenly sense depended on the order of words in a sentence and English arrived at a favoured order of subject-verb-object. Certain groupings of words into phrases (called 'collocations') became so standard as never to be questioned. For instance, adjectives follow an unwritten rule of order and, though we may speak of 'a good old man', we would never think of saying 'an old good man'. Inversions in word-order, such as 'Much have I travelled in the realms of gold' are reserved for poetry and rhetoric. Old English nouns also had gender, but that has completely disappeared, saving us all the trouble that speakers of other languages still have in remembering whether an inanimate object is a *he* or a *she*. By the sixteenth century we had decided that anything inanimate was an *it*, and thus made an end to it.

The church at Stoke Poges, Buckinghamshire, where Thomas Gray is buried in a brick-built tomb beside that of his mother. Reflections in this churchyard led Gray to write a poem which is now invariably cited as an example of the use of the iambic pentameter

The Curfew tolls the
    knell of parting day,
The lowing herd winds
    slowly o'er the lea.
The plowman homeward
    plods his weary way,
And leaves the world to
    darkness and to me.

THOMAS GRAY: Elegy in
a Country Churchyard

I am ready to praise the measureless making
That in foreshadowing and seeking
Formed place and light, for all creation's sharing,
Those things without beginning yet begun,
By God-love given, by potency upholden.
The unimaginable, shaped in substance,
In eternity made time's companion,
World and earth-kind by God's grace guarded.
I am small to pray such Fathering,
Unknowable God, perfect in persuasion,
Of all wonder the awakener,
Who out of inward wanting spun the heavens,
Gave the body of space a heart for living
and called it Earth, in water and air life eager,
Under tides, or wings clouding the brightness
And creatures warm in their ways, the day possessing,

The secret night invading, speed and strength
And lightness herald in a marvel of muscle.

Then the spirit of God moved across the world
Like a man's breathing and disturbed the dust.
The dust heard, stirred as a moon rising,
Came together in recognition. The dust saw.
The breath went in and out like the visiting of friends,
And the dust knew. Then the hands of God
Clapped amongst the clouds, clear water sprang
Ringing from the rocks, and the dust spoke.
There was Man, there was word in the world.
And from the neighbourhood of his heart
Eve took life, flower and fruit of the rib-stem.

CHRISTOPHER FRY: One Thing More, or Caedmon Construed

The way he created a speech was a wonderful bit of creativity. It was exactly like a director of a great orchestra. He would march up and down using his cigar as a baton, trying out different words for their rhythm, discarding some, whispering to himself, but when he finally got their rhythm, he would go on with his speech. It was like seeing a great piece of music. People supposed that he was naturally an orator but he wasn't. It came from the hardest work I've ever seen.

PHYLLIS FORBES, war-time secretary to Winston Churchill (from an interview)

Something which appears to govern the English is the belief that what we have is not necessarily the best. This idea has given birth to many traits, such as a national lack of self-appreciation on one hand and on the other an openness to trial, experiment and change. It is this idea which has caused the language to develop in the way it has for, as the grammar declined, so the vocabulary increased, and much of its increase came from abroad. Most European languages are content with a basic store of words and resist foreign incomers (particularly English ones: guardians of the French language rail at such abominations as *le weekend*). One of the habits of the English, however, is to pick up anything useful or beautiful from anywhere and make it their own, be it philosophy, religion, laws, words, or merely everyday things such as garden plants and cookery recipes. Although not every word taken in has been fully assimilated, most have become so English that the average speaker has no idea that they might ever have been anything else. *Pleasure, leisure, fashion* and *passion*, all of which near enough dominate society today, are French words and French concepts. *Eggs, legs,* and the *sky* came with the Vikings, although obviously they came as words only. We already had the concepts, and some names for them, but many Old English names lost out to Old Norse ones.

An examination of English vocabulary can, like a cross-section of a tree, reveal the history of the nation. At the core is Anglo-Saxon with its Germanic and Indo-European roots. Then we have a faint ring of ecclesiastical Latin from the seventh century, followed by a grainy ring of words accumulated from the Danes, a substantial ring of French and then a secondary and much fuller ring of Latin, shot through with Greek. At the outer edges of recent times, we have modern English, a

Whitby Abbey, Yorkshire, was originally founded by Hild in 657 but the ruins remaining today date from the 13th century

product of all that has gone before along with much accumulated since from all the nations of the world.

The Christian missionaries of the seventh century brought with them words such as *bishop* and *church*. Englishmen such as Bede became literate in Latin and wrote in it, but Anglo-Saxon remained the language of poetry. To reach the level of genius, art stands on the shoulders of popular participation. The highest peaks rest on the broadest bases. When Shakespeare wrote his masterpieces, for instance, sonnet-writing was the pastime of many. The level of language in Anglo-Saxon poetry reveals a society revelling in the spoken word. Not only the professionals enjoyed tuning their speech to a high pitch: wherever men gathered by the fire, a harp would be passed round and, on its reception, a man might tell a tale as best he could.

When the Celtic and Roman churches were debating unity at the Synod of Whitby, at that monastery was a stableman called Caedmon. He was bashful of hearthside gatherings, believing himself inadequate in speech. Then one night in his sleep he was blessed with an angelic vision in which he was given the gift of poetry. 'Poetry' in those days did not mean the crafting of a sonnet in romantic seclusion; it meant the public recital of a tale in the thumping good rhythms of the storyteller. To face a demanding, discerning, educated audience requires nerve, and Caedmon had it not until his angel came. Once graced, however, he turned his new talent in a new direction and sang in praise of the bestower of the gift. Caedmon's *Hymn to Creation* was the first child of the marriage between the Anglo-Saxon language and Christianity. While the theologians of the Synod deafened themselves

in debate, the Holy Ghost they had invoked was heard only by the man in the cow-byre. Caedmon's poem, the stable-born child of the union of English and Christianity, was the true product of Whitby.

Thanks to the work of book collectors such as Sir Robert Cotton, much else survives of Anglo-Saxon poetry, including the epic *Beowulf* and *The Battle of Maldon*. In Anglo-Saxon poetry, which continued to be composed until the period of Norman ascendancy, we discover the concerns of a warrior caste and, it has to be said, we can often hear what is a familiar sound of glumness. The hero of *The Wanderer* was not a happy man, but then the English have never had happiness at the top of their list of national priorities. The dominant sound of Anglo-Saxon poetry is reflective gravity. Nymphs and shepherds came to English poetry on that fifteenth century wave of Mediterranean influence called the Renaissance. The preferred form of English poetry, to which it returns again and again, is that of natural speech and natural subjects. Although Anglo-Saxon poetry used a refined form of language with a special vocabulary, it still had within it the very Englishness of English speech. Indeed, it was a language shared by all the kingdoms of England before there was one nation and one unified everyday language.

Mutable and malleable, English is particularly prone to changes in sound, called 'vowel-' and 'consonant-shifts'. At some point in the Anglo-Saxon period we gained the lovely sounds of *sh* and *ch*, the men wore shirts rather than skirts, went to sea in ships rather than skips, and to church rather than to the kirk. The Vikings brought a return of the hard sound, so that we now have both in our sound range. The Scandinavians who occupied the north of the country, arriving via their

So they stood by Panta's stream in proud array,
the ranks of the East Saxons and the host from the ash-ships,
nor might any of them harm another
save who through arrow-flight fell dead.

The flood went out. Eager the fleet-men stood,
the crowding raiders, ravening for battle;
then the heroes' Helm bade hold the causeway
a war-hard warrior – Wulfstan was his name –
come of brave kin. It was this Ceola's son
who with his Frankish spear struck down the first man there
as he so boldly stepped onto the bridge's stonework.

THE BATTLE OF MALDON, from the Anglo-Saxon,
AD 991 (trans. Michael Alexander)

settlements in Dublin and the Isle of Man, seemed to be received more happily than those in the south, and Viking and Anglo-Saxon villages grew up beside each other. Whitby itself was never called that during the time of the Synod. Then it was 'Streanhalch' – a name more fitting for a bad case of catarrh. Whitby or 'White village' is its Viking name. Thwaites and Thorps are Viking; names ending in -ton and -ing, Anglo-Saxon. During the absorption of the Scandinavians by the English, the language indulged its self-enriching habit of acquiring synonyms. Examples include wish and want, craft and skill, and skin and hide. The Anglo-Saxons had the concept of *word-hoard* as language to be drawn upon; we will extend the metaphor and consider the word-hoard as a treasury of vocabulary. Using every opportunity to add to the store, our forefathers began accumulating a treasure which would eventually make English the richest language in the world.

The Danes were settled on the eastern side of the country by the treaty drawn up between Alfred and Guthrum. From near defeat Alfred had rallied the English against the Vikings. To get the English together in opposition was no easy matter at a time when 'England' was still several kingdoms. Alfred used the language itself as his means of creating a sense of national identity. No doubt he could wield a sword to make a Viking tremble, but it is as a master of language that he is revered today.

For most of his life Alfred nurtured the ambition of learning Latin but the Vikings never gave him any peace. After the treaty was signed, he had ten years for his work. Straightway he gathered to his court those few men, Mercian, Frankish and Welsh monks, who were scholars in Latin, and had himself educated. At the age

And the force inspiring them [English poets] is love, controlled by reason; not rhetoric controlled by timidity; nor correctness controlled by cynicism.

ROBERT GRAVES:
The Crowning Privilege

of forty he mastered Latin, not so that he might read books for his own benefit, but so that he might translate them into English for the benefit of all his people.

During that decade he and his scholars translated St Gregory's *Pastoral Care*, *The Consolation of Philosophy* by Boethius, and Augustine's *Soliloquies*. He was at work on the Psalter itself when he died. His choice both of works and of the words with which to translate them reflect a philosophic rather than a theological approach to Christianity. Alfred was not a man of devotion and piety so much as a disciple of Wisdom. For him, knowledge was the way to God.

In his translations he made a decision that would affect the course of the English language. Where appropriate, he would translate 'sense for sense' rather than word for word. Whether he knew it or not, he was choosing between English and Latin speech rhythms, and was opting for English. Later scholars, particularly during the Renaissance, would contort English sentences into semblances of Latin ones. Alfred, when he wrote, wrote it plain; therein lies his genius, and that of those who have followed him.

Simplicity is the greatest art in writing. In simplicity, the natural rhythms are allowed their freedom. Alfred's English was simple and whenever anyone speaks of 'good, plain English' they have in mind an ideal born of Alfred. It is a prose which Churchill used when he told the nation that 'We shall fight on the beaches; we shall fight on the landing grounds, we shall fight in the fields and in the streets, we shall fight in the hills; we shall never surrender.' Each word in that famous sentence, bar the last, is English in origin. Plain English is not for anyone whose intention is to evade, baffle or impress, be he politician, small-print writer or businessman. The

basic English sentence structure of subject – verb – object is for those who wish to say what they mean and to impart their thoughts with the utmost clarity.

Just as the tribal territories of Anglo-Saxon England were forming into one nation, there came the invasion of those Vikings who had occupied northern France, the Northmen or Normans. For as much as the Normans spoke French badly they spoke it insistently and for a century or more the English language suffered the same oppression as the English people. Language, any language, requires careful nurture if it is to retain whatever purity it may have, and those members of society to whom it falls to act as the guardians of language are the poets, scholars, lawyers and officers of state. During the Norman period that level of society was occupied by French speakers, a fact that is still obvious in the language of the law. The Anglo-Saxon Chronicle, which had been instituted by Alfred, was abandoned in 1154 and English, between the eleventh and thirteenth centuries, was left to the care of the folk. Even then great literature was not entirely absent; mystical and devotional works, such as *The Ancrene Riwle*, shine out of the darkness. In general, however, the great and noble language of the Anglo-Saxons became the tongue of the peasantry, for whom 'fine words butter no parsnips'.

Ignorance is the prime enemy of language; the natural tendency to mimic the use of words and not to wonder about their true meaning has led to many words in current usage having a very different if not opposite meaning from the one first intended. *Silly*, for example, once Old English for happy, now means daft, a definition we will all understand even though *daft* once meant meek and mild. Similarly, when the speaker is unsure of the grammar, he will fudge it and smudge it

I often wonder if I did not know English, what I should think of the sound of it, well talked. I believe I should esteem it a soft speech, very pleasant to the ear, varied but emphatic, singularly free from gutteral or metallic sounds, restful, dignified, and friendly. I believe I should choose it, well spoken, before any language in the world, as the medium of expression of which we would tire last. Blend though it be, hybrid between the two main stocks, and tinctured by many a visiting word, it has acquired a rich harmony of its own, a vigorous individuality. It is worthy of any destiny, however wide.

JOHN GALSWORTHY: On Expression

and swallow the ending. The English today, even though their words are already truncated, still tend to mute the endings. Any English person who has struggled to speak French, Italian or German knows the horror of having to pronounce a word fully, clearly and with confidence in order to be understood. To speak a foreign language requires a muscular effort strange to the English tongue. There is no doubt about it: the English are lazy in the area of the tongue, and the laziness began in the neglect of language in the early Middle Ages.

Language needs constant tuning and refining by those who are expert in it. In the period before *The Canterbury Tales* and *Sir Gawain and the Green Knight*, English had precious little of such attention. But it was deep-rooted, ancient, and had its own genius still. As enmity grew between France and England, and the Anglo-Normans had to choose their nationality, English began to be heard again in high places. Anglo-Normans such as Simon de Montfort and Bishop Grosseteste spoke out in it and for it, denouncing the Frenchness of the court of Henry III. The first king since the Conquest to speak English was the one Shakespeare chose to embody the spirit of the nation: Henry V. If Henry really did rally his troops once more to the breach, he did so in their own language. No wonder they loved him.

The humanist Renaissance of the fourteenth to the sixteenth centuries had a great effect on all the languages of Europe. On the one hand, the study of classical literature by scholars introduced a flood of new terms; on the other, and more curiously, those same scholars with their fine new appreciation of Latin and Greek worked to develop their own vernacular tongues into languages of literature. Italian in particular flourished in the care of men such as Petrarch and Dante. But the

As I remained in the Third Fourth three times as
long as anyone else, I had three times as much of it
[English Analysis under Mr Somervell]. I learned it
thoroughly. Thus I got into my bones the essential
structure of the ordinary British sentence – which
is a noble thing. And when in after years my
schoolfellows who had won prizes and distinction
for writing such beautiful Latin poetry and pithy
Greek epigrams had to come down again to
common English, to earn their living or make their
way, I did not feel myself at any disadvantage.
Naturally I am biassed in favour of boys learning
English. I would make them all learn English; and
then I would let the clever ones learn Latin as an
honour, and Greek as a treat.

WINSTON CHURCHILL: My Early Life

English humanists inherited a language that was not only Germanic in origin, and
therefore not amenable to classical forms and constructions, but was also the poor
starved child that had been locked in the dark during the centuries of Norman
overlordship. The man who, through his genius for language, was to raise English
back to the level of literature was Geoffrey Chaucer; he did it by borrowing all that
was useful from French, Italian and Latin, while yet staying true to the language of
his fellow Englishmen. No-one knows why it was that Chaucer, whose writing
career began at the time when the French courtly romance was the most popular
form of literature, chose to work in his native language. It may have been that he
was following his Italian contemporaries, Petrarch, Dante and Boccaccio, in using
the vernacular, or it may have been in response to the political mood of the nation
after the English victory at the Battle of Crecy. But perhaps it is a mistake to think
that one of the most important moments in the history of English is due to a
decision made by a poet; Chaucer being a true poet, it is more likely that he was
chosen by the language rather than the other way round. Through him the
Germanic and French elements were harmonized into one language. And if that was
not enough achievement for one lifetime, through his translation of *The Consolation
of Philosophy* by Boethius, Chaucer was the main conductor of neoplatonic
philosophy into England during the Middle Ages. This philosophy, which sees Man
as divine in essence, has underwritten the development of England and the English
in more ways than is commonly realized, as will be seen in subsequent chapters.
Here suffice it to say that its transmission in England has been the work not so
much of great teachers or philosophers as of poets.

Until the fifteenth century, Plato was known in the west mainly through the book of Boethius, as well as a few fragmentary quotations accessible only to scholars. It was the work of Italy to bring the *Dialogues* to Europe, and the work of the Florentine Marsilio Ficino to translate them from Greek to Latin. That monumental event made Boethius redundant. The next poet to act as chief servant of the language and to speak it into a new form had the benefit of living in a culture which had access to Plato in the original.

By Shakespeare's time the language was again undergoing major changes. What grammatical inflections had survived in Middle English were all but gone while the humanist Renaissance had imported a massive amount of Latin into English speech. Some of Shakespeare's more pedantic contemporaries complicated matters further by trying to import latinate niceties of grammar and to make English conform to foreign rules. The various attempts to latinize sentence structures were made without regard to what was natural and euphonic. Once again the nation was splitting between the aristocrats who spoke one kind of language and the common people who spoke another. A new poet was required to restore unity and the genius of Shakespeare, like that of Chaucer, was his ability to turn a bi-lingual vocabulary into one language of renewed and vital power.

In the Renaissance England's long apprenticeship in word-adoption came to fruition. Any word that was useful and amenable, English could and did take in. To the word-hoard, already enriched by Danish, French, ecclesiastical and scholastic Latin, many new words began to be added. The study of ancient literature gave the humanists two vast sources of new words. Up to this time, words of Latin derivation

Go, litel book,
And for ther is so gret
    diversite
In Englissh and in writyng
    of oure tonge,
So prey I God that no
    myswrite the,
Ne the mysmetre for
    defaute of tonge.

CHAUCER: Troilus and Criseyde

92

Now entertain conjecture of a time
When creeping murmur and the poring dark
Fills the wide vessel of the universe.
From camp to camp, through the foul womb of night,
The hum of either army stilly sounds,
That the fix'd sentinels almost receive
The secret whispers of each other's watch.
Fire answers fire, and through their paly flames
Each battle sees the other's umber'd face;
Steed threatens steed, in high and boastful neighs
Piercing the night's dull ear; and from the tents
The armourers accomplishing the knights,
With busy hammers closing rivets up,
Give dreadful note of preparation.
The country cocks do crow, the clocks do toll,
And the third hour of drowsy morning name.
Proud of their numbers and secure in soul,
The confident and over-lusty French
Do the low-rated English play at dice;
And chide the cripple tardy-gaited night
Who like a foul and ugly witch doth limp
So tediously away. The poor condemned English,
Like sacrifices, by their watchful fires
Sit patiently and inly ruminate
The morning's danger; and their gesture sad
Investing lank-lean cheeks and war-worn coats
Presenteth them unto the gazing moon
So many horrid ghosts. O, now, who will behold
The royal captain of this ruin'd band
Walking from watch to watch, from tent to tent,
Let him cry 'Praise and glory on his head!'
For forth he goes and visits all his host;
Bids them good morrow with a modest smile,
And calls them brothers, friends, and countrymen.
Upon his royal face there is no note
How dread an army hath enrounded him;
Nor doth he dedicate one jot of colour
Unto the weary and all-watched night;
But freshly looks, and over-bears attaint
With cheerful semblance and sweet majesty;
That every wretch, pining and pale before,
Beholding him, plucks comfort from his looks;
A largesse universal, like the sun,
His liberal eye doth give to every one,
Thawing cold fear, that mean and gentle all
Behold, as may unworthiness define,
A little touch of Harry in the night.

SHAKESPEARE: Henry V

93

The house where William Shakespeare was born in Stratford-upon-Avon

had trickled into English through the church and through French. Now they flooded in, joined by Greek derivatives for the first time.

The ability of Chaucer and Shakespeare to make the language sing arose from their understanding of the secret of its strength: a simple native grammar and a multiplicity of words. The flexibility of the language, and its readiness to be moulded into a million different forms, allowed them to portray humanity as it is: essentially simple but in appearance infinitely variable.

The studies of classical literature of the humanists, plus the opening up of the world, added thousands of new words to the word-hoard. Not all these words were foreign borrowings. Many were coined in a cultural atmosphere of verbal inventiveness. The same culture caused many old words to perform new tricks. Nouns were used as verbs and verbs as nouns; adjectives and adverbs enjoyed equal abandon. Suddenly words such as *carpet*, *bed*, *foot*, and *fall* could be both activities and things.

Writers felt free to add English endings to Latin roots, and Latin endings to English ones. Thus suffixes such as -able and -ability were used to produce such words as *unutterable*. Making verbs with endings like '-ify' allowed Shakespeare to come up with a line such as 'o flesh, flesh, how art thou fishified!' (Romeo and Juliet). Coining new words became a popular pastime in Elizabethan and Jacobean England, but not all the spawn became tadpoles, and not all the tadpoles became frogs, and not all the frogs became princes, but many did, when kissed by popular acceptance.

The inrush of Latin terms, along with rhetorical tropes and figures of speech,

Holofernes. He draweth out the thread of his
verbosity finer than the staple of his argument.
I abhor such fanatical phantasimes, such
insociable and point-devise companions; such
rackers of orthography, as to speak 'dout' fine,
when he should say 'doubt'; 'det' when he
should pronounce 'debt'- d, e, b, t, not d, e, t.
He clepeth a calf 'cauf', half 'hauf'; neighbour
vocatur 'nebour'; 'neigh' abbreviated 'ne'.
This is abhominable – which he would call
'abbominable'. It insinuateth me of insanie:
ne intelligis, domine? to make frantic, lunatic.

Moth. They have been at a great feast of language
and stol'n the scraps.

Costard. O, they have liv'd long on the almsbasket
of words. I marvel thy master hath not eaten
thee for a word, for thou are not so long by
the head as honorificabilitudinitatibus; thou
art easier swallows than a flap-dragon.

SHAKESPEARE: Love's Labour's Lost

*Lampost donated to
Stratford-upon-Avon
by the State of Israel*

led some Renaissance writers into the flowery thickets of false speech. Others, particularly those who were governed by having something important to say, avoided foppish phrases and made natural, spontaneous English their mainstay. In using the resources of the language to the full they found that, with the useful addition of thousands of foreign terms, English could now convey subtleties not possible in many other languages; found, in fact, that English could act as a medium for truth.

To speak truly one requires freedom of expression and, while all truthful speech is poetic, not all poetry is truthful. English does not lend itself to rhyme (*teacup* still seeks its match). With the great influx of French and Latin vocabulary, however, came the fashion for it. This, along with the desire for metrical verse forms, put constraints upon English poetry which, from time to time, tend to strangle it, contorting the grammar and rendering diction artificial. It is to Henry Howard, Earl of Surrey, that we owe the two forms of poetry which, while remaining classical in structure, allow the English voice to express itself both naturally and with great dignity. These are blank verse and the sonnet. Blank verse, which is based on iambic pentameters but does not rhyme, became the preferred means of expression of the Elizabethan dramatists, including Shakespeare. And it was Shakespeare, of course, who was to take the sonnet to perfection.

Although Milton followed the Howard line and wrote *Paradise Lost* in blank verse, by the eighteenth century English poetry was enslaved to rhyming verse and was alienating anyone who had not enjoyed a classical education. It was not until the nineteenth century that there was a reaction and Wordsworth called for a return to

95

Though I speak with the tongues of men and of angels, and have not charity, I am become as sounding brass, or a tinkling cymbal. And though I have the gift of prophecy, and understand all mysteries, and all knowledge; and though I have all faith, so that I could remove mountains, and have not charity, I am nothing. And though I bestow all my goods to feed the poor, and though I give my body to be burned, and have not charity, it profiteth me nothing.

Charity suffereth long, and is kind; charity envieth not; charity vaunteth not itself, is not puffed up. Doth not behave itself unseemly, seeketh not her own, is not easily provoked, thinketh no evil; rejoiceth not in iniquity, but rejoiceth in the truth, beareth all things, believeth all thinks, hopeth all things, endureth all things.

I Corinthians 13: 1-7

'the real language of men.' Since then, the best of the English poets have written poems accessible to all and, in someone like T. S. Eliot, we may even hear an echo of the Anglo-Saxon bards whose rhythms still pulse in the language when it is free from affectation.

No matter how influential Shakespeare was, his works were never daily reading for the population as a whole and it is to the translation of the Bible that we owe the development of English into the language we now speak. The rebellious habit of translating the Bible into the English language began early. With the first translation appearing fifty years after the death of Alfred. One theory states that the Norman invasion, which had papal blessing, was mounted almost as a crusade to bring the unruly English back into line and the Bible back into Latin. If so, the effort ultimately proved to have been in vain. A contemporary of Chaucer, John Wycliffe, produced a translation of the Gospels and this act of heresy was followed by that of Miles Coverdale and Walter Tyndale. It was Tyndale's translation of the Gospels of 1536 that was to form the basis of the Authorized Version in the reign of King James.

The effect of Tyndale upon the language cannot be overstated: his words and phrases are the very marrow of modern English speech, and he arrived at them by his study of Hebrew. The rhythms of the Bible are Hebrew rhythms and therefore some of the rhythms of modern English are Hebrew rhythms, but Tyndale, like the translators of the Authorized Version, chose his words from the native stock, from Anglo-Saxon. Thus in the Authorized Version, over ninety per cent of the words used are native English, this at a time when to pepper one's speech with foreign

... the English Bible should be studied by us all for its poetry and its wonderful language as well as for its religion – the religion and the poetry being in fact inseparable.

ARTHUR QUILLER-COUCH:
On the Art of Reading

With the words came the things

spices was the mark of an educated man, and the translators were nothing if not educated.

 As English blossomed at home, it began to spread abroad. The age of discovery had two-way traffic. Europeans sailed the oceans in a fever of acquisition, but while other nations heaved home gold from the New World, the English brought home potatoes, tobacco and new words. In return they introduced settlers to the Americas with a language more catching than any Spanish disease. The Plymouth settlers were astonished to find that some of their native neighbours already spoke English: the natives had picked it up from the crews of merchant trading ships. American English established itself in the fashion of its parent. Even before the settlers had settled, they were adding words such as *wigwam*, *racoon*, *squash* and *mugwump* to the lexicon, and were as happy to call a patch of land *Massachusetts* as *Virginia*.

During the period of the British empire, more words piled into the hoard. From all over the world we gathered what was useful: *bananas*, *tigers*, *pyjamas*, *kangaroos* and *budgerigars*. With the words, of course, came the things. Word and concept come together. You cannot have one without the other.

Reflecting the mood of his age, Milton's nephew published *The New World of English Words* in 1658. The invention of printing, followed by the publication of dictionaries, served to standardize spelling. All the early dictionaries were of new or difficult words but Nathan Bailey's *An Universal Etymological English Dictionary*, which appeared in 1721 with a list of about forty thousand words, was more

One species of goatsucker cries, 'Who are you? Who are you?' Another exclaims, 'Work away, work away.' A third, 'Willy, come go, Willy, come go.' A fourth, 'Whip-poor-Will, Whip-poor-Will.' It is very flattering to us that they should all speak *English*!

SIDNEY SMITH: Book review of 'Wanderings in South America' by Charles Waterton, Edinburgh Review 1826.

The house on the corner of the market-place, Lichfield, where Samuel Johnson grew up

inclusive. The most famous dictionary, however, was that of Dr Samuel Johnson who, at the time when the French had forty scholars labouring for forty years to compose a French dictionary, compiled his English one in four years with the help of a couple of assistants. In so doing, he made himself a national hero. Like all good Englishmen, Johnson was cavalier with rules, and freely added to his serious compilation definitions such as:

> Lexicographer – A writer of dictionaries, a harmless drudge
> Oats – A grain, which in England is generally given to horses, but in Scotland supports the people.

Johnson sought to give the best 'usage' of a word and to do so resorted to one hundred thousand quotations from literature. In 1836 Charles Richardson complained that Johnson had failed to define words chronologically, had ignored their root meanings and the development of their sense through the ages. To correct this he defined 'the historical principle'. This, in effect, was the rule of precedent which is so fundamental to English common law, and it became the basis of the greatest of all dictionaries. *The Oxford English Dictionary* represents another fine English tradition, that of voluntary work. Without the free assistance of readers set to mine the canon of English literature for quotations, the cost of publication would have been prohibitive. This work of staggering authority, this product of earnest Victorian philology, this enormity which, when micrographically condensed into two volumes, weighs 20 lbs and has to be read with a magnifying glass, begins thus: 'If there is any truth in the old Greek maxim that a large book is a great evil, English dictionaries have been steadily growing worse ever since their inception more than

His next instructor in English was a master, whom, when he spoke of him to me, he familiarly called Tom Brown, who, said he, 'published a spelling-book, and dedicated it to the UNIVERSE; but I fear no copy of it can now be had.'

James Boswell: The Life of Samuel Johnson

three centuries ago'.

There is no truth in the old maxim, and the second edition, which appeared in 1989, is in twenty volumes, contains over six hundred thousand words and cites almost two and a half million quotations. As the preface to the first edition said, 'no one man's English is *all* English,' and it would probably be fair to say that the majority of these words are of little use to most people. But there they are, all available, and comprising together one nation's potential for expression.

Though the richness and exoticism of our vocabulary lies in the realm of nouns and verbs, it is all the little words, taken so much for granted, that are the very Englishness of English (this sentence has twenty-one of them). While most of the words in the dictionary are foreign, most of the words of speech are native and, though we can form a sentence without using a foreign word, we cannot form one without using a native word. The core language is the structure by which we embrace the rest of the world and all the knowledge of mankind. Words are concepts and with over six hundred thousand of them in our lexicon, if we do not already have available to us every concept known to man, at least we have the means and tradition for acquiring them. This vocabulary, with its aptitude for expressing subtle shades of meaning, makes English an unequalled vehicle for world communication. Where once the scholars of the world spoke to each other in Latin, today the scientists, mathematicians, doctors, artists and statesmen speak in English. An estimated eighty percent of the world's population now speaks some English and English itself must have words from at least as many of the world's languages. A random search through the *Concise Oxford Dictionary*, which lasted only

The spider population of an acre of grassland may be as much as 2,000,000. Under certain weather conditions, particularly warm sunny mornings in autumn, these spiders are stirred into uneasy wanderings. They cover the grass stems, hedges, and railings. Each trails a thread as they walk; so, in due course, the whole field may be covered with a shimmering silver sheet. I call this vast concourse 'a smother of spiders'. Gossamer is the result.

Dr W.S. Bristowe, Entomologist and Etymologist (quoted by Ivor Brown: Chosen Words)

In 1989 Oxford University Press closed down its printing house, the Clarendon Press, and rebuilt the site for use as editorial offices. The new Clarendon wing was designed by AMEC and completed in 1993

five minutes, revealed the following exoticisms: *savoir-faire*, *diwali*, *chickadee*, *tarentella*, *seraglio*, *serape*, *sannyasi*, *bludger*, *farucca*, *bongo* and *bonze*, all of which are fascinating but none of which will be of any use in the writing of this book.

The habit of adopting foreign terms and collecting synonyms comes easy to the English: it is the natural thing to do, even if it leads to clutter. This, plus the other English habit of distorting a pure vowel into several impure ones, has put a great strain on the alphabet.

The first Anglo-Saxons wrote little and were content with a runic alphabet of sixteen letters with which to inscribe memorials and graffiti. In fact the alphabet was considered mysteriously potent and its use a ritual of sympathetic magic (which is still performed every time a child etches a beloved name on the school desk). It was never foreseen by our ancestors that the written rather than the spoken word would be the medium for learning. Writing, when it was invented in Mesopotamia, was required merely as a memory-aid. By the time of the Roman Empire, however, writing had become the very tool of learning, and literacy was the first requirement of an educated man. When the Celtic Christians introduced the English to the Latin alphabet, a relationship between speech and writing began that was to become as barmy as it is endearing. Though the Anglo-Saxons managed to be consistent in spelling, by the time of Chaucer it was all but out of control. People readily blame English for having an illogical and difficult system of spelling, but much of the problem lies in having an alphabet which does not fit. The sound-values of the Latin letters are comparatively pure and simple. The Latins, after all, do not combine their consonants into tongue-clutching clusters. It was left to scribes and scholars to select certain combinations of letters to reproduce Teutonic sounds. To show how arbitrary these choices often were, consider that the sound *-dge* was in Old English signified by *-cg* and thus what is now *bridge* was once spelt *brycg*; despite looking unpronounceable to modern eyes, it was in fact pronounced the same. How letters sound is a matter of common consent. Latinate speakers (with the exception of the French) have the advantage of comparatively pure vowel sounds and consistent spelling whereas, at the latest count, there are twenty-three English vowels: fourteen simple vowels ('Who would know aught of art must learn, act, and then take his ease') and nine doubles and triples ('Fear the poor outside the door; beware of power, avoid desire').

Most of these sounds are not vowels at all but are distortions from the seven pure sounds on which all speech is based ('Oh, I see how to make you laugh', pronounced in southern English). It is probable that we have not exhausted the possibilities for queerly pinched or stretched sounds and there may be more to come. The latest linguistic development in English is a form of pronunciation called 'Estuary English', a hybrid resulting from a cross-fertilization of Cockney with middle-class 'standard' pronunciation. It was born in south-east England around the Thames estuary, possibly as a result of the mingling of the 'barrow boys and Harrow boys' in the City of London in the 1980s. Popularized by politicians and TV personalities, it is now spreading across the country.

With all these obstacles to simplicity, it is hardly surprising that so many people – and not only foreigners – find English difficult to learn, however easy its grammar. The only possible way to gather the *sound* from the *spelling* is through the use of the International Phonetic Alphabet, which alone can show on paper what happens in speech. George Bernard Shaw famously shamed English orthography by pointing out that 'fish' may be logically spelt as 'ghoti': *gh* as in 'laugh', *o* as in 'women', *ti* as in 'nation'. Of course everyone knows that 'ghoti' does not spell fish but goaty, but that knowledge stems more from common sense, or rather common agreement, than from any set of rules. But the English being English, and despite objectors such as Shaw and Anthony Burgess, they resist the IPA, and are right to do so. The spelling of a word, however illogical it may appear, is the only way to connect with the rich and varied history of the language and its people.

Merton College Library, Oxford, founded in the fourteenth century

Since the Industrial Revolution the dialects of England have been dying out and, since the onset of broadcasting, they have almost expired, but there is still a great variety of regional pronunciation. In the Middle Ages that variety was greater still, but one area came to dominate the others. The English of Chaucer (Middle English) is that area of the east Midlands known as the 'golden triangle', covering as it does the area between Oxford, Cambridge and London. However, the accent of that area is no longer the same as in the fourteenth century when it was but one of many regional accents. Today, thanks to public-school education, to broadcasting, and above all to the very idea of a 'regionless' accent, the golden triangle is now the centre of what is known as 'received pronunciation' or 'BBC English'. Reaching its heyday during the colonial period, received pronunciation has recently diverged into two streams, 'advanced' and 'modified

The headquarters of the BBC, beside All Souls, Langham Place, London

regional'. The Royal Family promotes the first, and the BBC the second. Received pronunciation has become accepted as the standard accent, particularly by other nations learning English, but it is not the most beautiful. Samuel Johnson considered that his neighbours in Lichfield, Staffordshire, spoke the best kind of English, and, indeed, Lichfield produced not only Johnson, but also the first editor of the Spectator, Joseph Addison, and the great Shakespearean actor David Garrick. And of course the neighbouring county of Warwickshire had been the home of Shakespeare. Any glance at the literary map of England shows that the location of the great users of the language does not necessarily correspond to the golden triangle. As for what is known as 'The (King's or) Queen's English', that is synonymous with standard English usage and not with pronunciation. English may be well-spoken in any regional accent and, were we to have a national competition for clear enunciation and musicality, the prize may well go to the descendants of the good yeomen of Johnson's Middle England.

The criteria for good pronunciation, as the criteria for standard grammatical forms and spellings, have like our laws been established by custom and precedent over long ages. Our dictionaries and grammars are guide books rather than rule books. In the end, the arbiter is common agreement. The English language is a free market. Rigid spellings and, even more so, rigid meanings, are the marks of a totalitarian society where semantics are state-controlled. A free market leads to a life of great variety and interest and allows the individual to make his own choices (and his own mistakes), but it is open to danger and abuse.

The English language still needs guarding, and guarding well. Change is

From the authors which rose in the time of Elizabeth, a speech might be formed adequate to all purposes of use and elegance. If the language of theology were extracted from Hooker and the translation of the Bible; the terms of natural knowledge from Bacon; the phrases of policy, war, and navigation from Ralegh; the dialect of poetry and fiction from Spenser and Sidney; and the diction of common life from Shakespeare, few ideas would be lost to mankind, for want of English words in which they might be expressed.

SAMUEL JOHNSON

It is inevitable, perhaps, that Latin – so long the Universal Language – would cease in time to be that in which scientific works were written. It was impossible, perhaps, to substitute, by consent, some equally neat and austere modern language, such as French. But when it became an accepted custom for each nation to use its own language in scientific treatises, it certainly was not foreseen that men of science would soon be making discoveries at a rate which left their skill in words outstripped; that having to invent their terms as they went along, yet being careless and contemptuous of a science in which they have not training, they would bombast out our dictionaries with monstrously invented words that not only would have made Quintilian stare and gasp, but would affront the decently literate of any age.

ARTHUR QUILLER-COUCH: The Art of Writing

Therefore a man never attains virtue and excellence through his power; rather he attains power and authority through his virtue and excellence ... Study wisdom, therefore, and when you have learned it, do not neglect it, for I say to you without hesitation that you can attain authority through wisdom.

KING ALFRED: Preface to the translation of Boethius *Consolation of Philosophy*

natural and inevitable. Speakers saying 'perceived' when they mean 'seen', or 'consensus' when they mean 'agreement' are only following an age-old tradition of using latinate terms when wanting to impress. Some of the new uses may stick, some may not. It seems incredible to us today that a word like *mob* was once objected to (being an abbreviation of *mobile vulgus*), while within living memory the use of 'once', once it became used as a conjunction, grated on fine ears. There will always be objection to every innovation but the language is a living thing and, though it needs looking after, it should not have, indeed cannot have, its growth stunted.

There is, however, a new use of the language that is more pernicious than the small errors of grammar and vocabulary which, when committed on the radio, have the BBC being deluged with letters of complaint. It is worth considering what the fate of the nation might have been if Sir Winston Churchill had tried to rouse us with the words 'whether the enemy-engagement is in a marine, terrestrial or agricultural situation, or even in elevated terrain, a no-win scenario is not on the agenda'. This modern political language, which has to be dissected for meaning – and sometimes you open the body of a sentence to find that its internal organs bear no relation to each other – is the language of those who have no desire to be understood. European unification is being founded on it. The Maastricht Treaty is written in it. It is a language which has to be translated – who knows how – into all the languages of the EU and NATO. Modern wars are called 'conflicts', genocide is 'ethnic cleansing' and by the use of language we are desensitized. Euphemism keeps us as removed from the reality of war as the electronic weaponry distances the warriors. It is the language of diminished responsibility. This world of calling a

The earth is not so dull; these eyes that see
See all too easily, and pass too swift
By things of wonder that would gently free
Our minds from sorrow and our souls uplift.
These old, old miracles seem far too worn.
A child alone feels their mystery's glow,
And sees the light in all things reborn;
These suns, for us, are darkened now. But lo,
The light is not dim; I see it shine
So clear and bright on my heart's great hill,
See the peaks of others reflecting mine:
This beauty is eternal and eternal still,
Though the sun be turned to a ball of rust,
And we and the world to shimmering dust.

JAMES PICKLES: Sonnet V

spade a gardening implement is a dangerous place.

In ancient folk tales, where there is treasure there is a dragon. The name of the dragon which has wrapped itself round our word-hoard is Jargon. Bent as it is on keeping us from the proper, rightful use of our fabulous store, Jargon has been clever: Jargon has become fashionable. In truth it is nothing but a florid, wordy disguise for, at best, flabby thinking, at worst, downright deception. It deserves the spear. Whenever an Englishman wants to speak the truth, the words he chooses will be drawn largely from the native stock, and his sentences will be clear and simple. King Alfred, the translators of the Bible, and Winston Churchill have all shared a preference for simple English.

Today, while playwrights persist in a postwar habit of negativity, while schoolchildren are being torn between different ideologies of learning, while all parties of government obfuscate speech to the point where the nation believes nothing that is said, there are some signs of hope. The lead, as ever, is being taken by the poets. A generation of egotistic, so-called 'free' verse has had its day and the new poets are returning to the old forms. Better still, there is a growing public interest in poetry and it is no longer the case that only poets read poems. This could be the first sign of a revival of learning, of oratory and of purpose in the nation. Similarly, as English spreads across the world, it meets with linguistic enthusiasm, particularly in India and the Caribbean. Taken together these may be signs of a renaissance and each English renaissance so far, whether in the seventh, tenth or sixteenth centuries, has been in the realm of language. The seed of any renaissance is the desire for truth. That alone unites men, transcending as it does divisions of race, religion and politics.

The poet's eye, in a fine
    frenzy rolling,
Doth glance from heaven
    to earth, from earth
    to heaven;
And as imagination bodies
    forth
The forms of things unknown,
    the poet's pen
Turns them to shapes, and
    gives to airy nothing
A local habitation and a name.

SHAKESPEARE: A Midsummer
Night's Dream

THE
OPEN-AIR
CHURCH

Therefore to the Light
I direct you, that with
it ye may see yourselves.

GEORGE FOX: Letters

*Uffington Castle on the
Ridgeway, Berkshire*

The sun, the moon, the stars, the seas, the hills and the plains —
Are not these, O Soul, the Vision of Him who reigns?

Is not the Vision He? tho' He be not that which He seems?
Dreams are true while they last, and do we not live in dreams?

Earth, these solid stars, the weight of body and limb,
Are they not sign and symbol of thy division from Him?
Dark is the world to thee: thyself art the reason why;
For is He not all but thou, that hast power to feel 'I am I'?

ALFRED LORD TENNYSON: The Higher Pantheism

'The best of our English wisdom, and our clearest visions of the invisible, are enshrined in our poetry. Our best poetry is generally serious, moral, and often definitely religious in its aim.' So said William Inge, Dean of St Paul's. The best of English poetry is so moral and spiritual that it is difficult to separate the history of language from the history of religion. The first known poem in English was the *Hymn to Creation* composed by Caedmon and the first novel was *The Pilgrim's Progress* by John Bunyan. The Authorized Version of the Bible achieved such superlative beauty of language that it holds the place next to Shakespeare in the literary heart of England. When a castaway on 'Desert Island Discs' is given, as well as the book of his choice, a copy of Shakespeare and the Bible, it can safely be assumed that it is the Authorized Bible and no other.

Donne and Herbert were priests in the Anglican tradition. Others such as Bunyan and Milton were nonconformists and independent. But many poets, Blake, Wordsworth and Coleridge among them, are not readily associated with any church at all. Yet all embody the English religious spirit and what differences there are seem to be but variations of the same music. It was William Inge who in a series of lectures delivered at Cambridge in 1925-6 identified that music. Strangely, it is not Christian in origin; Christianity itself is but a recent expression of a tradition which has been singing in the world since man, if not time, began.

Dean Inge called it 'the platonic tradition', although Plato himself was just another singer, and not the composer. This tradition, which forms the mystical aspect of English religiosity, is easily overlooked amidst all the blood and thunder of English Church history. That history is one of conflict, be it between the Roman and Celtic Churches, between Protestant and Catholic, between 'Low' Church and 'High' Church, or between one Nonconformist sect and another. It is a history of debate, dispute, torture and trial. It is a political history, and it has little (perhaps nothing) to do with true religion. But whenever a man or a woman seeks God, the experience is a universal one, to be shared by any other individual engaged in the same quest. And therefore in these pages we celebrate what Inge calls the 'Religion of the Spirit' in its several voices, careless of the caste or colour of the speakers.

Inge called this tradition 'Platonic' and 'Spiritual' in order to distinguish it from ecclesiastical tradition. It has, he says, 'never been extinct; the fire has a perennial power of rekindling itself when conditions are favourable. But the repressive forces of tyranny and bigotry have prevented the religion of the Spirit from bearing its proper fruits. The characteristics of the tradition are a spiritual religion, based on a firm belief in absolute and eternal values as the most real things in the universe, a confidence that these values are knowable by man, a belief that they can nevertheless be known only by whole-hearted consecration of the intellect, will, and affections to the great quest, an entirely open mind towards the discoveries of science, a reverent and receptive attitude to the beauty, sublimity, and wisdom of the creation, as a revelation of the mind and character of the Creator, a complete indifference to the current valuations of the worldling.'

This tradition is at the heart of most of the world's religions. That it was known to the Indo-European tribes of deep antiquity is evident in the Vedic texts of India. When the Christian missionaries first moved amongst the pagan Anglo-Saxons, they were speaking of a strange prophet, but the prophet's words found

True religion is about love and sacrifice, about wisdom and justice, about hope and happiness, about God.

WILLIAM REES-MOGG:
The Times II February 1993

their echo in the pagan soul. The various tribes that composed the early English nation shared in the cult of Nerthus, the Mother Goddess. Theirs was a religion of nature and the roof of their church was the sky, its floor the earth. It was the religion of sacred groves and island sanctuaries. That it had much in common with the religious culture of Egypt and Babylonia, as well as with Judaism and Greek mythology, is due to two reasons. One is that during the ages of migration our forefathers had picked up influences from these cultures; the other is that all these cultures shared the same origin in the religion of the Indo-Europeans. The first great flowering of the spiritual tradition in recorded history was in the fifth century BC, the time of Lao Tsu in China, Zoroastra in Persia, and Socrates in Greece. The principle of unity which was common to these teachings was re-expressed in the words and work of Jesus.

 For the Christian seed to be sown across Europe, it took the Roman plough. Wherever the Romans went, Christianity sprang up behind them. But the Romans never conquered the Germanic nations, and the Angles, Saxons, Jutes and Frisians, although aware of Christianity, remained true to their ancient rites and beliefs. When they invaded Britain, which by this time was largely Christian, they came as full-blooded pagans, with all their kings elected from those that claimed descent from the god Woden.

The conversion of the English to Christianity began at the end of the sixth century with the arrival of Augustine and his monks at Canterbury. They were the forerunners of Rome's second attempt to civilize the land. We have to thank

(Listen! I will tell the best of dreams,
That I dreamed in the dead of the night,
When the speech-bearers were at rest.)
It seemed to me that I saw a wondrous tree
Born aloft, bathed in light,
Brightest of beams. All that beacon was
Covered with gold. Gems stood
Fair at the earth's corners; likewise there were five
Up on the crossbeam. A multitude of angels beheld there,
Fair from the beginning of creation; it was no felon's gallows.
But there beheld it holy spirits,
Men throughout earth, and all this glorious creation,
Wonderful was that victory tree …

THE DREAM OF THE ROOD, Anglo-Saxon,
before AD 750 (trans. Katharine Watson)

Set in one of the wildest areas of England, Bewcastle Cross is a fine example of Northumbrian art from the age of Bede. A similar Anglo-Saxon cross at Ruthwell, Dumfrieshire, bears the runic version of the poem 'The Dream of the Rood'

Augustine, and his successor Theodore of Tarsus, for the establishment of schools of Latin and Greek in Kent, but the rest of the story is a political rather than a spiritual one. Their work was to set up bishoprics and sees and to establish the Church in England. They met with limited success.

It was from the north, in the beginning of the next century, that the renewal of spirituality came. British, mystic Christianity had been transplanted to Ireland by the Romano-Briton, St Patrick. It returned to the mainland with St Columba and his monks who established their monastery on the Hebridean isle of Iona. And it was to Iona that Oswald, King of Northumberland, fled during dynastic wars.

Celtic Christianity had its roots in the desert hermitages of Egypt rather than in the city of Rome. Monasticism was the way of perfection, an austere lifestyle with the purpose of subduing the senses so as to know the immanence of God. It arose in reaction to orthodox Christianity which, as it gained widespread acceptance, became worldly and lost some of its integrity. Those who wished to follow the way of perfection chose to withdraw from society and to live the ascetic life of the hermit. By the fourth century, the deserts of Asia Minor and Egypt were attracting large numbers of both men and women. One man called Antony, less extreme and more rational than many of his fellow desert-dwellers, attracted a large following. This was the beginning of monasticism. Brought to Europe by St John Cassian, defined by St Benedict in his Rule, promoted by Pope Gregory the Great, monasticism flourished for as long as it could live in the shelter of the organized church. Whenever it became organized itself, however, it waned.

Celtic Christianity was entirely monastic. It had monasteries rather than

churches, and whenever its abbots were offered the office of bishop or archbishop, they tried to avoid it. It is hardly surprising then that it was no match for the competition from Rome, but neither was it annihilated. It became absorbed by the authoritarian, established Church, to become manifest again in the Middle Ages in the new monastic orders and the mystics. But meanwhile, in seventh century Britain, it had some space to grow, unrestrained by dogmatic stricture. When Oswald assumed his Northumbrian throne after the battle of Heavenfield, he sent to Iona for a monk to come and teach his people the new religion. An Irishman called Aidan was the only one brave enough to accept the challenge, and he established his monastery on Lindisfarne, an island under the protection of Oswald's royal hall at Bamburgh.

Lindisfarne, or Holy Island, is a crescent-shaped spit of sand dunes linked to the mainland by a causeway twice a day at low tide. The preference of the Celtic Church for offshore sites for their monasteries points the difference between the Celtic and Roman ways of devotion. For the Celtic monks, religion was a private matter, best conducted in peace and seclusion. Teaching was done by way of example. Aidan used the tides to balance his days between active work amongst the peoples of Oswald and retiring in prayer. The Angles could not help but be impressed. In Aidan and his followers they saw men who chose poverty above worldly riches, who moved in response to the will of God, who acted in total obedience to that will, and who lived as they preached. By word and by example the monks spoke to something deep in the Anglo-Saxon soul, something which had been covered over by generations of war and insecurity, an ancient teaching which

had begun to degenerate into superstition and folklore. Where Augustine's torch had met damp grass in the south, Aidan's met dry brush in the north. Northumberland, put to the torch, sent up flames, and from that fire came the first European renaissance of the Christian era.

The increasing attraction of the people to Lindisfarne soon made the island seem busy and overpopulated. Aidan retreated further to one of the nearby Farne Islands, which could only be reached by a small boat nosing its way stoutly through the choppy grey waters of the kingdom of seals.

When Aidan died in 651, a young Anglian shepherd called Cuthbert in what is now the Scottish lowlands was out all night watching the sheep when he saw a great stream of light breaking through the sky. Hearing on the following day of the death of the Abbot of Lindisfarne, and linking his angelic vision to the event, he set out to become a monk. He went to the monastery at Melrose, and it was many years before Cuthbert was to arrive at Lindisfarne and fulfil his role as spiritual successor to Aidan. His story is one of a man who is content to follow God's will and not carve out his own future. Eventually, of course, he became Bishop of Lindisfarne and, like Aidan, he too retreated to Inner Farne, the place that is now a sanctuary for puffins, guillemots, cormorants and shags.

According to Bede, 'The Farne lies a few miles to the south-east of Lindisfarne, cut off on the landward side by very deep water and facing, on the other side, out towards the limitless ocean. The island was haunted by devils; Cuthbert was the first man brave enough to live there alone … Having routed the enemy, Cuthbert became monarch of the place, in token of which he built a city

Seest thou not how graciously he hath pulled thee to the third degree and manner of living, the which is called Singular? In the which solitary form and manner of living thou mayest learn to lift up the foot of thy love, and step towards that state and degree of living that is perfect, and the last state of all.

CLOUD OF UNKNOWING: Anon, 14th century (spelling modernised by Katharine Watson)

... when we compare the present life of man
on earth with that time of which we have no
knowledge, it seems to be like the swift flight of
a single sparrow through the anqueting-hall where
you are sitting at dinner on a winter's day with
your thanes and counsellors. In the midst there
is a comforting fire to warm the hall; outside,
the storms of winter rain or snow are raging.
This sparrow flies swiftly in though one door
of the hall, and out through another. While he is
inside, he is safe from the winter's storms; but after
a few moments of comfort, he vanishes from sight
into the wintery world from which he came. Even
so, man appears on earth a little while; but of what
went before this life or of what follows, we know
nothing. Therefore, if this new teaching has brought
any more certain knowledge, it seems only right
that we should follow it.

BEDE: A History of the English Church and People

I need to understand the
nature that is in all things.
Stone is wood, water,
earth, and grass.

ANDY GOLDSWORTHY (sculptor)

worthy of his power and put up houses to match. The structure was almost circular in plan, from four to five poles in diameter, and the walls on the outside were higher than a man ... so that with only the sky to look at, eyes and thoughts might be kept from wandering and inspired to seek for higher things. This same wall he built not with cut stone or bricks and mortar but with rough stones and peat dug out of the enclosure itself.'

To have the roof open to the sky may only partly have been to keep the mind from wandering: it is a mark of English religiosity that it flourishes best without walls. If Nature is God made manifest, then the fact that more people prefer a walk in the countryside to sitting on a pew and listening to a sermon is hardly to be wondered at. Likewise, Cuthbert's disdain for well-dressed blocks of stone reflects an attitude which equates architecture with ostentation. Architecture was not going to grace the English Church until the English were under Norman rule, yet it was to be England that would be home to the first of the great cathedrals of Europe.

Durham Cathedral was built by the Normans in the twelfth century. Architecturally it resembles the castle built at the same time a matter of yards distant, yet there is a spirit to the Cathedral that is almost tangible. It is like a benign and gentle air which softens the impact of the powerful architecture upon the senses. A name has been given to this *genius loci*, which has been experienced by many people, and that name is 'Cuthbert'. This experience is not confined to impressionable authors or ardent Christians: Rabbi Lionel Blue, searching in his youth for holy England, found Cuthbert at Durham and, in him, a step in his own spiritual development.

The nave,
Durham Cathedral

It was during the Viking invasions that monks escaping from Lindisfarne took with them the coffin of Cuthbert, the head of King (now Saint) Oswald, and some illuminated manuscripts. At first the community resettled at Chester-le-Street, but further Viking inroads had them seeking a new refuge. Durham, a hill almost encircled by the River Wear, provided a natural fortress. It provided no protection, however, against the Normans.

Following the Conquest, ecclesiastical authorities began putting English saints under trial. Tombs and reliquaries were forced open and the authenticity of their contents challenged. When, as so often happened, the saintly remains failed to pass the strict tests for miraculousness, they were relegated to the charnel house. Thus were the English saints deposed. When the tomb of Cuthbert was opened, however, the Norman inquisitors found the body uncorrupted. The saint looked as if he were merely asleep. He was reburied with ceremony, along with the head of St Oswald, in a shrine behind the altar of the new Cathedral.

At the opposite end of the building, in the Galilee Chapel, is the tomb of the Venerable Bede. Between Bede and Cuthbert lies one of the most powerful pieces of architecture in all Europe. For those who have ventured north via the airy, delicate cathedrals of Lincoln and York, built in a later age, the first sight of the interior of Durham is staggering. Here the pillars, made of great drums of stone, are monumental, with crude patternings that seem to have been chiselled by giants.

The architecture of Durham cathedral was the first heavy step towards the sublime grace of the gothic style which was to transform the cathedrals of Europe. The great innovation for which Durham was the experiment was the construction

of a roof with rib-vaulting. Apart from anything else, this construction allowed for much larger windows than had previously been possible and light began to take its place as an element of architecture. Durham Cathedral now shares with the pyramids, the Taj Mahal and Versailles the designation of 'World Heritage Site'.

Cuthbert, celebrated by Bede and invoked by Alfred in battle, was England's saint until the canonization of the last Anglo-Saxon king, Edward the Confessor. Edward's cult saw England through the period of Norman dominance until, in the age of romance and chivalry, it was displaced by the somewhat esoteric cult of St George. But it is Cuthbert, whose living presence has been sensed by many, who is the true patron saint of England. At least the people of the north think so. The people of the south have barely heard of him.

The written lives of Cuthbert are in the usual, now almost unacceptable, style of hagiography. The modern mind balks at miracles and searches for other reasons as to why this man was special. An answer may be found in his indifferent response to an event which affected all the monastic communities of England: the Synod of Whitby in 664. In a council held to reconcile the differences between the Celtic and Roman churches, which had differing dates for Easter and differing shapes of tonsure, the Celtic side was debated by the then Bishop of Lindisfarne, Abbot Colman. He lost. Refusing to submit to Roman discipline, Colman returned to Iona. Cuthbert, brought up in Celtic ways and now prior at Lindisfarne, had remained aloof from the ecclesiastical disputes. Now he quietly accepted the decision of the Synod and dedicated himself to calming his ruffled brethren. To Cuthbert it simply did not matter what shape the tonsure was, or what the date of

Easter. He was of the kind who would rather practice the teachings of the Gospels than debate them. By his example his brethren were shown the true way of reconciliation.

Whitby was one of several monastic centres in the north east which were in effect religious villages. The scribes of works such as the Lindisfarne Gospels lived in barn-like huts in Jarrow, Wearmouth and Flixborough. The monasteries were often double monasteries, home to both men and women and presided over by an abbess: the Celtic Church had an enlightened sense of the capabilities of women and, while an abbess might not give the sacraments, she could govern a community. The nature of her role was summed up some centuries later by Dame Julian of Norwich in the words 'This fine and lovely word Mother is so sweet and so much its own that it cannot properly be used of any but Him.' Whitby was under the rule of the abbess Hild. In the Synod, Hild had sided with Colman. When he lost she, like Cuthbert, loyally accepted the Synod's decision, even though it was to change her world forever.

It was at Hild's Whitby that Caedmon had his visionary, pentecostal dream. Graced with the gift of poetry, Caedmon sang in praise of the Creation with the wave-power of Anglo-Saxon rhythms; he sang to the sound of the North Sea as it beat upon the cliffs below the monastery. The Celtic Church was never equipped to challenge the authority of Rome in the political arena; is it a coincidence that, at the very time it lost its place in the world, its voice began to be heard in poetry?

If there was any lingering sense of division between the Celtic monks and the Roman missionaries, it was healed in the work of the man known as the 'Father

Be thou, then, O thou dear
Mother, my atmosphere;
My happier world wherein
To wend and meet no sin;
Above me, round me lie
Fronting my froward eye
With sweet and scarless sky;
Stir in my ears, speak there
Of God's love, O live air,
Of patience, penance, prayer;
World-mothering air, air wild,
Wound with thee, in thee isled,
Fold home, fast fold thy child.

GERARD MANLEY HOPKINS:
Mary Mother of Divine Grace,
compared to the Air we breathe

of English History'. Bede was born nine years after the Synod of Whitby. When, at the age of seven, he was sent to the monastery at Wearmouth, it was to become a monk of what was now firmly the Roman church. Bede's literary language was Latin, and his regard for church discipline total, but in him the two streams of influence became one. In his writings, whether a man was from the Roman or Celtic tradition made no difference: it was a man's virtue that Bede respected, not his dogma.

Two years after entering the monastery at Wearmouth, Bede was transferred to Jarrow, where he was to remain for the rest of his life. He seems not to have travelled any farther than Lindisfarne in the north and York in the south. Towards the end of his life, encouraged by Abbot Albinus of Canterbury, Bede began assembling material for his *History of the English Church and People*. His desire to find the true history of the Anglo-Saxons, their arrival in Britain and their conversion to Christianity, and to record accurately what facts he could glean from both written sources and living witnesses created a work which defies time. The book can hardly be said to be typical of eighth century literature: neither chronicle nor hagiography but a history in the classical manner it reads well in any age and remains to this day the best guide to the early history of the Anglo-Saxons.

Bede had, in modern terms, a team of researchers at his disposal: Abbot Albinus provided the information about the Church in Kent; Nothelm of London, when in Rome, researched the papal archives for material relevant to the mission of Augustine; Bishop Daniel of the West Saxons offered material on Wessex, Abbot Esius on East Anglia, and the monks of Lastingham on Mercia. Thus, in his monastic seat on the banks of the Tyne, Bede drew in all the information he could gather from all the kingdoms of England; he drew into himself all the tales and the stories of miracles, all the fables and the facts, he digested it all within himself. When he begun to write, by adhering to what he considered to be true, he left out all that was untrue and produced a work that produced a nation. *A History of the English Church and People* rests on the premise that, despite its various kingdoms – Anglian, Saxon, Mercian and Jutish – England was a nation; that, despite its various laws, customs and dialects, its people were one. According to this book, and perhaps for the first time, those peoples were called by the one name *Angle-kynn*, their language by the one name *Englisc*. He ended the book with an account of life in 731 when, under Christian influence, the warring kingdoms were putting their weapons aside. It seems that Bede might have hoped, if not expected, that the future would be one of peace in which religion, literature and the arts might flourish.

Grave marker found at Lindisfarne, Northumberland. While the carver may have been evoking Doomsday as cited in Matthew 24:6, he undoubtedly had the Viking raid of 793 in mind

His lifetime corresponded with what is now known as 'The Golden Age of Northumbria', an age which produced the greatest treasures of Anglo-Saxon art, including the Lindisfarne Gospels. From that culture came Alcuin, a monk of York who went to the Franks as advisor to Charlemagne. At Charlemagne's court at Aachen (Aix-la-Chapelle), Alcuin founded a school of Latin and Greek studies which so lifted the culture of the Franks as to inspire what is called the Carolingian Renaissance.

This golden age was brought to a sudden end when, in 793 and again in 875, Lindisfarne was sacked by Vikings.

One hundred and fifty years later, the Northumberian scholar-monks must

The Alfred Jewel, 9th century, gold and cloisonné *enamel on rock crystal, now in the Ashmolean Museum, Oxford*

have seemed as remote as mythical heroes to the English people who, after generations of war, had forgotten entirely their Latin and Greek. Doubtless much Anglo-Saxon literature was also lost in this period. What books were left had become meaningless – the painstaking calligraphy of monks just so many inscrutable glyphs. This was the people that Alfred the Great was to lead back to the light. His revival of learning was based on his idea of what England had achieved in the eighth century. Of the many books he required to be translated into English, that they might never be lost again by being in a tongue alien to the English people, was Bede's history.

As Alfred aimed to revive learning, so did he try to revitalize monasticism. He sent copies of his books to bishops, along with bejewelled pointers called *aestels* which the readers could use to direct the eye to the words. The famous Alfred Jewel, found at Athelney, is thought to be the head of such a pointer. It bears the figure of Christ and is inscribed *Aelfred mec heht gewyrcan* ('Alfred had me made').

Among his many translations from Latin into English was that of *The Consolation of Philosophy* by Boethius, which picks up the golden thread of platonism, that thread which is only visible when the sun catches it. In his devotion to wisdom, Alfred was as Socratic as he was Christian.

It sometimes seems as if all the great figures in the nation's history belong to a club. Bede brought Pope Gregory the Great to the English; Alfred translated works by both Gregory and Bede; Bede wrote of Cuthbert, and was eventually interred in the same cathedral as the saint; Alfred's men invoked Cuthbert on the battlefields; Alfred translated Boethius, so did Chaucer; Chaucer wrote about

And yet, nevertheless, it behoveth a man or a woman, that hath long time been used in these meditations, wholly to leave them, and put them and hold them far down under the cloud of forgetting, if ever shall he pierce the cloud of unknowing betwixt him and his God.

Therefore, what time that thou purposest thee to this work, and feelest by grace that thou art called of God, lift then up thine heart unto God with a meek stirring of love. And mean God that made thee, and bought thee, and that graciously hath called thee to this work; and receive none other thought of God. And yet not all these, but if thou list; for it sufficeth enough a naked intent direct unto God, without any other cause than himself.

And if thee list have this intent lapped and folden in one word, for shouldest have better hold thereupon, take thee but a little word of one syllable; for so it is better than of two, for ever the shorter it is, the better it accordeth with the work of the Spirit. And such a word is this word GOD or this word LOVE. Choose thee whether thou wilt, or another as the list; which that thee liketh best of one syllable. And fasten this word to thine heart, so that it never go thence for thing that befalleth.

This word shall be thy shield and thy spear, whether thou ridest on peace or on war. With this word shalt thou beat on this cloud and this darkness above thee. With this word thou shalt smite down all manner of thought under the cloud of forgetting. Insomuch that if any thought press upon thee to ask thee what thou wouldest have, answer him with no more words but this one word. And if he proffer thee of this great learning to expound thee that word and to tell thee the conditions of that word, say him that thou wilt have it all whole, and not broken nor undone. And if thou wilt hold thee fast on this purpose, be thou sure he will no while abide. (And why? For thou wilt not let him feed him on such sweet meditations touched before.)

CLOUD OF UNKNOWING: Anon 14th century
(spelling modernised by Katharine Watson)

Troilus and Cressida, so did Shakespeare. A line has been established throughout the ages, a line of recurring themes, a double helix which is the hidden code of the English.

The Church which Alfred reinvigorated was the Roman Church, and the language of Christianity was Latin. With the coming of the Normans, the vernacular language of scholarship became French, but the English tongue was never quite silenced. English continued to be voiced from pulpits, in the simple, straightforward sentences which are its strength. One of the major pieces of religious prose of the period is the *Ancrene Riwle*, a set of devotional texts written for a group of anchoresses. The texts, which instruct on the way of Love through control of the senses, are pure monasticism, and were to be of great inspiration during the Tudor period when the Church was once again riven in two.

Mediterranean catholicism could never suit the English spirit for long and in the English of the Middle Ages we begin to hear again that free, independent voice that cannot be content with a religion imposed from abroad. The English tried their best to be devoted to Mary and the baby Jesus, but were never wholehearted in it. The Celtic saints, who were men of wisdom rather than martyrs, were supplanted by saints of the Roman calender, but these never fully captured the English heart and imagination. English religiosity centres on God himself and concerns the direct relationship between Man and his Creator. It is in the nature of intercessors to be in the way. The remarkable work, the *Cloud of Unknowing*, even treats all the orthodox reflections, generally expected of one who has chosen the religious life, as

'Knowest thou about a saint,' said they, 'that men calleth Treuth?
Could'st direct us the way whither out Treuth dwelleth?'
'Nay, so me god helpe,' said the man then,
'I saw never pilgrim with staff and bag
Asking after hym, but now in this place.'

'Peter!' said a plowman, and put forth his head.
' I know hym as kyndely as clerk doth his bokes.
Conscience and Reason kenned me to his place.
And maden me promise since to serven hym for ever.
Both to sowe and to plant the while I work hard.
And so sowen his seed, keeping his beasts,
Indoors and outdoors to care for his interests.
I have been his foloware al this fourty wynter
And served Treuthe indeed, somewhat to paye.
In alle kinds of craftes that he could devise
Profitable as for the plough, he potte me to lerne,
And, tho I say it myself, I serve him to paye.
I have myne age of hym wel and other whiles more.
He is the promptest payer that any pore man knoweth;
He with-holds no man his wages beyond dusk.
He is as meek as a lamb and loyal of speech.
And who-so wants to know where that Treuthe dwells,
I will direct you wel right to his place.

WILLIAM LANGLAND; Piers Plowman (C text, slightly modernised)

unwanted distractions. If we want to know God, it says, then we must meditate on Him alone.

The fourteenth century was the age of Richard II and John of Gaunt, of the Black Death and the Peasant's Revolt. It was the age when the struggle for freedom began to break down the old feudal structures of society and when the villein began his transformation into Everyman. Two men of the age spoke out against prevailing hypocrisies in the spare language of fearless protest. One was William Langland, the other John Wycliffe. In *Piers Plowman* we have Everyman challenging his contemporaries as to their sincerity. Rather than find a Christ figure amongst the clergy, Langland finds him at work in the fields.

It was the view of Wycliffe that if Christianity was the religion of all men, then it should be written in Everyman's language. Such an opinion, from a master of Balliol, was tantamount to heresy, but Wycliffe enjoyed the protection of the same man who was the patron of Chaucer: John of Gaunt. The Lancastrian duke who was father to generations of English monarchs seems to have been instrumental in England's rediscovery of herself. Whether this was done consciously or unwittingly is unknown, but under his protection and through the language, English spirituality was rekindled.

English spirituality is a queer thing, not well understood even by the English themselves. It begins with two feet planted firmly on the ground. It is strongly moral and firmly based on reason. When Wycliffe stated that wicked popes and bishops should not be in power, he was only stating the obvious. This gruff sense of natural justice is the foundation of the English church. Only when his faith is

The ruins of Rievaulx Abbey, Yorkshire

grounded by reason will the Englishman allow it to take him on the journey beyond the senses and the intellect.

The same century, so lively in the staring face of death, produced many hundreds of mystics and, amongst them, four great writers: Richard Rolle of Hampole (*The Fire of Love*), Walter Hilton (*The Ladder of Perfection*), Dame Julian of Norwich (*Revelations of Divine Love*) and the deliberately anonymous author of the *Cloud of the Unknowing*. Each of them, along with Langland, Wycliffe and all the great writer-teachers since, begin their journey in the here and now. It is a journey that begins at home.

In Langland's poem is an extraordinary prophecy of what was to follow two centuries later. The feudal society was a long time breaking down. One of its faults was to put monastic abbots in the position of landlords. Whatever the affront to the aesthetic sensibilities of the nation made by the dissolution of the monasteries, it cannot be doubted that the monasteries brought it upon themselves. Even in the story of Ailred of Rievaulx, who lived in the twelfth century, we see an early print of the pattern that was to dominate the medieval world.

Son of a Saxon priest of Hexam, Ailred was steward in the Scottish court of King David, the court that had harboured the refugees from the Royal House of Wessex after the Norman Conquest. While in England on the business of King David, Ailred came across a secluded valley in Yorkshire in which was an abbey of the newly founded Cistercian order. The history of monasticism is a cyclical one of growth, decay and renewal, and the Cistercians, followers of St Bernard of Clairvaux, were seeking to re-establish the purity of the sixth century Benedictine Rule. Ailred

Also in this he showed a little thing, the quantity of an hazelnut in the palm of my hand; and it was as round as a ball. I looked thereupon with eye of my understanding and thought, 'What may this be?' And it was generally answered thus: 'It is all that is made.' I marvelled how it might lasten, for methought it might suddenly have fallen to nought – it was so little. And I was answered in my understanding: 'It lasteth and ever shall, for god loveth it; and so all thing hath being – by the love of God.' … It needeth us to have knowing of the littlehead of creatures and to noughten all thing that is made for to love and have God that is unmade.

DAME JULIAN OF NORWICH: Revelations of Divine Love (modernised by Katharine Watson)

But now is Religion a rider a roamer of streets,
A leader of love-days and a land-buyer,
A rider on a palfrey from manor to manor,
A heap of hounds at his heels as though he a lord were.
And unless his knave kneels when he brings him his cup
He lours on him and asks him who taught him his manners?
The lords ought not to give land from their heirs
To men of Religion, who though pity rains on their alters, have none.
In many places where high persons are they live at their ease;
Of the poor they have no pity and that is their charuty.
But they forsake them like lords their lands lie so broad.
But there shall come a king and purge you men of Religion
And beat you as the bible telleth for breaking of your Rule,
And put them to their penance *ad pristinum statum ire.*

WILLIAM LANGLAND: Piers Plowman (modernised by Katharine Watson)

was moved by his visit to give up his worldly career and enter the monastery as a novice. He soon rose to be abbot.

It cannot be proved from the little of his writings that remain, but there are various clues which show that Ailred was politically active, and that his purpose was the healing of a nation divided between Norman and English. In his genealogy of kings, for instance, he takes pains to give Henry II English origins. It seems that while Becket was stealing the limelight, Ailred was busy behind the scenes. Yet even this great man's history bears the taint of landlordism. He may have given up his own worldly goods, but he made keen plans for the enlargement of the monastery. Such enlargement required taking land from others, and was part of the building grudge that was to erupt in the Peasant's Revolt.

In becoming landlords, the abbots lost touch with the original intention of their order. Ironically Spirit was to return with those men of the Renaissance who steeped themselves in pagan literature.

 The cultural flowering which in Italy manifested itself in the arts of painting, sculpture and architecture, in England chose the realms of literature and language. Although deriving its inspiration from medieval France, which in turn had derived its inspiration from Anglo-Saxon England, Italy was the earliest place of this flowering in the accepted time span of the fourteenth to the sixteenth centuries. England took on the New Learning with a new king, Henry VII. His mother, Lady Margaret Beaufort, had educated herself and her son in the tradition of the Italian humanists. She founded various chairs at both Oxford

and Cambridge, though it is Cambridge which particularly reveres her, and was the patron of many English humanists.

In the person of John Colet, a precursor of Inge as a Dean of St Paul's, we have a man who, like Wycliffe, chose the Bible rather than its commentaries as his source material. Like Wycliffe, he was of Oxford University; unlike Wycliffe, however, he was not trained in theology. It was as a Bachelor of Arts that he had travelled to Italy, where he made contact with Marsilio Ficino, the founder and father of the neoplatonic school of Florence, and it was as a man with a mission that he returned. Through a vivid series of lectures on St Paul, he strove to turn the University from sterile intellectualism to the disciplined and practical approach of the early Church. Along with two other Oxford men, Thomas Linacre and William Grocyn, Colet was among the first to learn Greek, and it was he who persuaded a Dutch Augustinian monk called Erasmus to stop his frivolous pursuits in letters and poetry and to do something useful. At the age of 34, Erasmus was bullied into a study of Greek and, later, into translating St Jerome. All Europe owes gratitude to Colet for that. Erasmus repaid his own gratitude by helping Colet to establish the first grammar school in England, that of St Paul's.

Another of Colet's circle was Thomas More. In accordance with his father's will, he had come to Oxford to study law but, after meeting Colet and Erasmus, he begged to be allowed to pursue a study of classical literature. His father refused and More was sent to the bar to begin a career which would lead eventually to him becoming Lord Chancellor of England. The men around Colet were concerned with purity of understanding of Christian scripture. Their thoughts were only with

Leave me, O Love, which reachest but to dust,
And thou, my mind, aspire to higher things!
Grow rich in that which never taketh rust:
Whatever fades, but fading pleasure brings.
Draw in thy beams, and humble all thy might
To that sweet yoke where lasting freedoms be;
Which breaks the clouds and opens forth the light
That doth both shine and give us sight to see.
O take fast hold! let that light be thy guide
In this small course which birth draws out to death,
And think how evil becometh him to slide
Who seeketh Heaven, and comes of heavenly breath.
Then farewell, world! thy uttermost I see:
Eternal Love, maintain thy life in me!

SIR PHILIP SIDNEY: *Splendidis longum valedico Nugis*

125

The gate-tower of St John's College, Cambridge, bears the emblems of the college's founder, Lady Margaret Beaufort, 'scholar, gentlewoman and saint'

reform of the Church, not with revolution. That was to come from abroad. Erasmus and Colet managed to steer their barque over the turbulent waters of the political intrigue that was the English Reformation; More did not.

John Fisher, Chancellor of Cambridge University and chaplain of Lady Margaret Beaufort, persuaded Erasmus to move to Cambridge. And it was in Cambridge, under the influence of Erasmus and the humanists Sir Roger Ascham and Sir John Cheke, that platonism took root.

The reigns of Henry VIII, Mary Tudor and Elizabeth I cover the most brutal, shameful period of the history of the English Church. These episodes of torture and executions reveal a darker side of human nature that sits ill in the story of religion. At last the storm abated and, following on from the work of Elizabeth and her advisers, the reign of James I saw in the Church a period of freshness and quiet in which certain minds could flourish.

Richard Hooker was born in 1554 in Exeter of a Protestant family. The family was poor and Richard's education was looked after by his uncle, John Hooker, who had been an editor of Holinshed's *Chronicles*. After grammar school, Richard went on to Corpus Christi College, Oxford, and began a career in the Church. At that time the Established Church was something of a mixed breed. It had retained the trappings of Catholic worship, including the ritual, vestments and liturgy, and to them had added a rather woolly Protestant theology. It was an organisation more political than spiritual in its essence and an easy target for the scorn of the Puritan party. It became Hooker's task to counter Puritan arguments and he did so in five books called *Of the Laws of Ecclesiastical Polity*. Despite the mustiness of its title, it is one of the gems of Anglian literature, a masterpiece of philosophy, and a channel for that quality which the English have so valued ever since: religious tolerance.

The central theme of his work was this, that man need not, as the Puritans claimed, judge everything against scripture, for man has been blessed by God with the instrument of Reason. By that he may judge for himself whether a thing is good or bad, right or wrong. To prove his point, Hooker examined the whole nature of law, government, society and man himself. The resultant work was a great reiteration of the Platonic tradition and a major inspiration not only to his contemporaries, such as William Shakespeare, but also to men of future generations such as Edmund Burke. Through Hooker's work, fledgling Anglicanism was brought into the timeless tradition of the Spirit, and, by his understanding of the unity of all things, and of the role of Reason, he reconciled the apparently contradictory beliefs of Reformation and Renaissance. As Christopher Morris has said in his introduction to the Everyman edition of the *Laws*, 'He had found a way to harmonize the variability of human institutions with the universality of law. He recognized man's need for government but also man's right to be governed only by his free consent. Above all, Hooker showed men how to philosophise without becoming doctrinaire, how to remain relatively tolerant and strikingly moderate in a fanatical world.'

Suddenly where there had been harshness and bitter dispute, a gentle sound began to run through English religion. Also there was renewed interest in that platonism which had inspired in Hooker such a generous vision. Whilst other philosophers of the time, such as Thomas Hobbes, tutor of Charles II, persuaded

All men desire to lead in this world a happy life. That life is led most happily, wherein all virtue is exercised without impediment or let.

RICHARD HOOKER: Of the Laws of Ecclesiastical Polity

the world to an entirely materialistic and mechanistic view of the universe, a group
of men centred on Emmanuel College, Cambridge, pursued platonic studies.
Benjamin Whichcote, Henry More, John Smith, and others of like mind held true to
the perennial belief of an invisible world of pure reason which sustains the physical
world. The torch which had been lit by Plato in the fifth century BC, which was
rekindled by the neoplatonists of Alexandria, by Duns Scotus, Anselm and Boethius
in the Middle Ages, by Ficino in Renaissance Florence and by Shakespeare and
Hooker in Elizabethan England, was passed on by the Cambridge Platonists to the
poets Wordsworth and Coleridge of the eighteenth century.

Meanwhile the history of the Church stumbled on, in a manner described
by Inge as 'not very encouraging to those who hope for better things from
organized religion … It is the story of a corporation growing rich and
powerful, not of a spiritual leaven gradually leavening the whole lump.'

The Church of England, or Anglicanism, was born from the Reformation and
its voice is heard purely in the poetry of George Herbert. He, with his friend
Nicholas Ferrar, relinquished worldly gain and honour to become simple parish
priests. The community Ferrar established at Little Gidding in Cambridgeshire in
1625 inspired T. S. Eliot to one of his greatest poems, *The Four Quartets*, which in
turn has inspired the re-establishment of the community in recent years. This early
Anglicanism was the church brought home. Herbert owed everything to his mother.
Of her he wrote:

Teach me, my God and King,
In all things thee to see,
And what I do in any thing,
To do it as for thee;

Not rudely as a beast,
To runne into an action;
But still to make the prepossest
And give it his perfection.

A man that looks on glasse,
On it may stay his eye;
Or if it pleaseth, through it passe,
And then the heav'n espie.

All may of thee partake;
Nothing can be so mean,
Which with this tincture ('for thy sake')
Will not grow bright and clean.

A servant with this clause
Makes drudgerie divine;
Who sweeps a room, as for thy laws,
Makes this and th' action fine.

This is the famous stone
That turneth all to gold:
For that which God doth touch and own
Cannot for lesse be tolde.

GEORGE HERBERT: The Elixir

To thee I owe my birth on earth / To thee I owe my heavenly birth /
As thou didst lead I followed thee / Thou wast a mother twice to me.

In the person of Magdalene Herbert we find Anglicanism at its sweetest and
most potent. Hers was the Christianity of the hearth and home and she taught her
son to see that the humblest task well done was work worthy of the Lord. Yet she
was also a lady of society and, at her table, George met Francis Bacon, John Donne
(who celebrated Magdalene in several sonnets), William Byrd, and Lancelot
Andrewes, one of the translators of the Authorized Version of the Bible. The lute
playing of Donne and Byrd gave Herbert the rhythms of his poetry, but the greatest
music was in the voice of Andrewes, who was Herbert's tutor at Westminster
School. As Ronald Blythe has said in *Divine Landscapes*, 'When Andrewes spoke, his
extraordinary ability to embue tradition with originality, causing old familiar things
to scintillate in the minds and emotions of his congregation, threw the conventional
worshipper off balance ... Both Queen Elizabeth and King James remained
fascinated by Andrewes as, year after year, at Christmas and Easter, and in a voice
and language which stunned their courts, he repeatedly set out before them the
huge tale of redemptive love. He was their Isaiah, learned, simple and eloquent
beyond belief.' When Herbert read the Old Testament in the Authorized Version,
he 'must have experienced the curious sensation of having a voice he had listened
to at his mother's table ... strangely in duo with the voice of the Creator himself.'

Andrewes was so skilled in classical and oriental languages that a
contemporary wished that he might have served as 'interpreter general in the
confusion of tongues'. Similarly, his knowledge of scripture was exquisite in its

Our Saviour made plants and
seeds to teach the people;
for he was the true
householder, who bringeth
out of his treasure things
new and old ... that labouring
people (whom he chiefly
considered) might have
everywhere monuments of
his Doctrine, remembering
in gardens, his mustard-seed,
and lillyes; in the field, his
seed corn, and tares; and so
not be drowned altogether
in the works of their
vocation.

GEORGE HERBERT:
A Priest to the Temple

Let mans Soule be a Spheare, and then in this,
the intelligence that moves, devotion is,
And as the other spheares, by being growne
Subject to forraigne motions, lose thier owne,
And being by others hurried every day,
Scarce in a yeare their naturall forme obey:
Pleasure or business, so, our Soules admit
For their first mover, and are whirld by it.

JOHN DONNE: Goodfriday

To everything there is a season, and a time
            to every purpose under the heaven:
A time to be born, and a time to die; a time
            to plant, and a time to pluck up that
            which is planted;
A time to kill, and a time to heal; a time
            to break down, and a time to build up;
A time to weep, and a time to laugh; a time
            to mourn, and a time to dance;
A time to cast away stones, and a time
            to gather stones together;
A time to embrace, and a time to refrain
            from embracing;
A time to get, and a time to lose, a time
            to keep, and a time to cast away;
A time to rend, and a time to sew; a time
            to keep silence, and a time to speak;
A time to love, and a time to hate; a time
            of war, and a time of peace.

ECCLESIASTES, 3:1-8

*Tomb of Lancelot
Andrewes in Southwark
Cathedral, London*

detail, and he instinctively used it to express anything he had to say. This man, whose life was full of scholarship, who performed copious duties to the court and church in his role as bishop, who set aside hours each day for private devotions, still found time for recreation. And his chief pleasure? – long, solitary walks in the countryside, where he could make close observations of nature in the church of the open air. From him, and from others like him, sprang the greatest book in the language.

The Authorized Version was not so much a translation as a revision or, as it calls itself, a 'version'. Fifty of England's top scholars in Greek and Hebrew sat in six groups at Oxford, Cambridge and Westminster. The Old Testament from Genesis to 2 Kings was given to Andrewes' group at Westminster; Oxford, under the leadership of Dr John Harding, had the Prophets. Poor Cambridge, stricken by the death of two of her translators, produced an indifferent version of the Psalms; thereafter the discerning have turned for the Psalms to Cranmer's Book of Common Prayer, the translations of which were based on those of Miles Coverdale.

Each group was given a section of the text on which they then worked. Their translations were generally revisions of earlier ones, and the voices of William Tyndale and John Wycliffe remain particularly audible. It was the purpose of the translators to return to the original Hebrew and Greek for correct rendering of the text, to retain old ecclesiastical terms such as 'church' for 'congregation' and 'baptism' for 'washing', and so to steer a middle course between Puritan and Roman versions. What the Jacobean translators brought to the work was greater poetry, for poetry was the supreme gift of the age which embraced Shakespeare. Also,

following all the work of the Renaissance scholars in the fields of Latin and Greek, they had an enormously enhanced vocabulary on which to draw. This allowed them to translate those words that repeated monotonously in the classical texts with a variety of English alternatives, and to avoid the baldness of a literal translation. Their spirited Renaissance approach was however tempered. Rather than follow the current fashion for verbal copiousness, they followed the earlier translations and thereby stayed true to the basic rhythm of English speech, giving us in the process such gems of idiom as 'by the skin of his teeth', 'a lamb to the slaughter', 'a drop in the bucket', and 'the apple of his eye'.

Each group having completed its task, it sent its work to another group for critical comment. Thus, in two years and nine months, the monumental work was ready for the press. In 1611 England was presented with its greatest of all treasures, a book which translated the Word of God in a language where a wealth of vocabulary was contained and controlled by native rhythm. In this work, the English language reached its maturity. And yet, though authorized by the King and beloved by the people, it was only ever 'appointed' to be read in churches and was never officially authorized by church authorities.

During this time, George Herbert was a student at Cambridge. It was after graduating that he gave up the chance of a career at court to become the vicar of a tiny, run-down parish in the fens, close to that of his friend Ferrar at Little Gidding. Herbert preached his first sermon in the baroque prose of a Cambridge scholar. After that dismal failure, he spoke to the ploughboys and labouring men in plain English. His poems, too, use the simplest language, and have the simple,

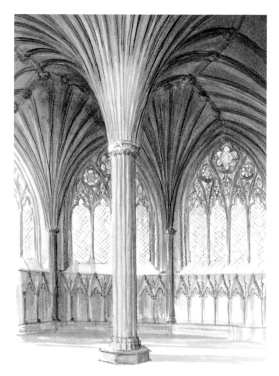

*The Chilterns at West
Wycombe. This and
similar scenes inspired
Bunyans's vision of the
Delectable Mountains*

Wells Cathedral, Somerset

harmonious rhythms of the quiet lute.

The sound of the lute ran behind English life of this period as the sound of a fountain in a garden, and it is perhaps in these centuries that English music found its own character. The English tend to assume that the greatest pieces of music have been written by foreigners and that we have never had a Mozart or Beethoven. Perhaps not, but we have had Byrd, Tallis and Purcell. In the Elizabethan Age, language and music often came together in sonnet and song. This lute and consort music, when translated into a sacred setting, retained its gentleness and quietude. English music, like English art, is watery, gentle and kind, and is capable of achieving sublimity without arousing the passions. One of today's leading composers John Tavener, like the best of his forebears finds inspiration in the sacred.

The new always springs naturally and spontaneously from the old whereas forced growth leads merely to the artificial and contrived. The various attempts to render the Bible into 'modern' English have succeeded only in denuding the Tudor version of its poetry. The Church argued that the language of the Authorized Version was alienating modern parishioners. The truth is that the lofty language of the Authorized Version was *always* remote. It was never, at any time, everyday language, for the translators never thought to present scripture in the language of broadsheet or chapbook. It was lofty language for a lofty subject, spoken to arouse the soul.

Poetry and religion run together in the person of John Milton, who was born four years after the conception of the Authorized Version. The son of a scrivener and composer of music, he was educated at St Paul's School and at Christ's College,

Then I saw in my dream, that on the morrow he got up to go forwards, but they desired him to stay till the next day also; and then, said they, we will, if the day be clear, show you the Delectable Mountains; which, they said, would yet further add to his comfort, because they were nearer the desired haven than the place where at present he was; so he consented and stayed. When the morning was up, they had him to the top of the house, and bid him look south. So he did, and behold at a great distance, he saw a most pleasant, mountainous country, beautified with woods, vineyards, fruits of all sorts, flowers also, with springs and fountains, very delectable to behold. Then he asked the name of the country. They said it was Immanuel's Land; and it is as common, said they, as this hill is, to and for all the pilgrims. And when thou comest there, from thence, said they, thou mayest see to the gate of the Celestial City, as the shepherds that live there will make appear.

JOHN BUNYAN: Pilgrim's Progress

Cambridge. Though he began writing poetry while at university, he intended to pursue a career in the Church, but this idea was abandoned when he found himself unable to follow the orthodox, dogmatic line of Anglicanism. Milton was a Puritan by inclination, but too independent to be a Puritan by definition; devoting himself to scholarship and writing, he never shied from speaking his mind. The Restoration ruined him both financially and politically, and the result was his greatest work, *Paradise Lost*. As a Nonconformist, as a man imprisoned for his beliefs, and as a master of language, Milton is the spiritual precursor of Bunyan, but in their backgrounds and particularly in their education, there is little similarity.

Born of a tinker family in Bedfordshire, John Bunyan educated himself by reading the Authorized Version. Through the influence of his wife, he joined a Nonconformist congregation at Bedford. He became a preacher whilst maintaining the family tinker business, hauling his anvil and tools round the parishes of the Chilterns. He was imprisoned in Bedford Gaol for twelve years for preaching without licence. Here he wrote extensively, the most famous of his books being his autobiography *Grace Abounding* and, of course, *Pilgrim's Progress*. His congregation, called The Bunyan Meeting, continues to this day in Bedford.

 Nonconformism is a blanket title for groups as disparate as the Quakers, the Baptists and the Methodists, all of which derive from the Church of England. The movement began during the Reformation with the Puritans who, in reaction to 'popery', went to extremes of severity, stripping the churches of all ornamentation, the priests of their vestments and offices, the services of their

Pendle Hill, Lancashire

liturgy. The puritanical whitewashing had an iconoclastic effect: it was in this period that we lost our medieval wall-paintings and carvings and reduced our medieval heritage down to a few illuminated manuscripts. The removal of bishops led to Presbyterianism or rule by elected elders. By the time of the Civil War and the Commonwealth, sects were proliferating, many of them beginning with one man finding fault with the others and setting himself up as a new model of pure living. Some, however, proved to be of lasting value.

During the years of Cromwell's rule, a young man wandered the Midlands looking for religious simplicity and spiritual direction. Confronted by the rising mass of Pendle Hill in Lancashire, he climbed it. It is an arduous climb, and the view from the wind-buffeted top is as spectacular as it is unexpected. George Fox found God on Pendle, and the world gained the Society of Friends, or Quakers.

With the Restoration of the monarchy in 1660 the Church of England was also restored, along with the bishops, the music and the vestments. The Act of Uniformity in 1662 required that all clergy use the revised Prayer Book and those that refused, about a thousand strict Presbyterians, were expelled from their livings. Siting themselves in villages beyond a five mile limit, they established their own congregations. Some of those exiles returned to London when, during the plague, the Anglican ministers fled and left their flocks to their fate. At the close of the plague, however, the Nonconformists returned to exile.

As the so-called Caroline Divines, Lancelot Andrewes, Jeremy Taylor and George Herbert, had arisen during the Reformation to remind people of the sweet essence of religion, so during the decline of the church into sects and factions came

And did those feet in ancient time
Walk upon England's mountains green?
And was the holy Lamb of God
On England's pleasant pastures seen?

And did the Countenance Divine
Shine forth upon our clouded hills?
And was Jerusalem builded here
Among these dark Satanic Mills?
Bring me my bow of burning gold!
Bring me my arrows of desire!
Bring me my spear! O clouds, unfold!
Bring me my chariot of fire!

I will not cease from mental fight,
Nor shall my sword sleep in my hand,
Till we have built Jerusalem
In England's green and pleasant land.

WILLIAM BLAKE: Milton

the Latitudinarians, John Tillotson and Edward Stillingfleet, as well as the Cambridge Platonists, to try and instil calm, restraint, courtesy and kindness.

After centuries of dispute and uncertainty, it is perhaps not surprising that the Church of England in the eighteenth century was torpid. While the deans and the canons complacently tended their roses or dined with squires, the Nonconformists in their country congregations found themselves to be adaptable to, and ready for, what was coming.

With the Industrial Revolution and the startling expansion of villages such as Birmingham or Middlesborough, the Nonconformist congregation became the usual form of worship in the new urban centres. Such meetings were the birthplace of modern democracy. In the newly built chapels and meeting houses, men learnt how to debate their opinions, how to moderate them, even abandon them when necessary; here men elected their officers; here men had a say in the organization of their communities. Appealing neither to the upper classes, who patronized the established Church, or to the very poor, who tended to opt for cynicism, the Nonconformist congregation became the spiritual vehicle for the middle classes and the rising economic phenomenon of capitalism.

Throughout the eighteenth century people moved from country to factory. A spiritual leader for the dispossessed arose in the form of John Wesley. Under the influence of mystics such as William Law and Henry More, Wesley had formed a study group at Oxford University. His first experience in preaching was against the slave-trade in America but it was only after he returned home that he had the conversion experience which led to the vow to 'promote as far as I am able vital

I have been this morning for a walk up the Langham Hills, and through a number of beautiful fields and by the side of the river — and in my life I never saw Nature more lovely ... Every tree seems full of blossoms of some kind and the surface of the ground seems quite lovely — every step I take and on whatever object I turn my eye that sublime expression in the Scripture 'I am the resurrection and the life' etc., seems verified about me.

JOHN CONSTABLE, Letter to his wife, May 1819

*The hexagonal Methodist
chapel at the weavers'
village of Heptonstall,
West Yorkshire,
established in 1742*

practical religion and by the grace of God to beget, preserve, and increase the life of God in the souls of men'. Wesley did not set out to found his own congregation: he was forced out of the Church he had had no mind to leave. He began field-preaching to colliers in 1739. He was tireless in his journeys around Britain, averaging eight thousand miles a year. By the time of his death, Methodism had thousands of members both in Britain and in America. Wesley must have presented the people with the undeniably attractive prospect of a man who practised what he preached. As the midland and northern towns began to choke in the smoke of the false promises of progress, the dispossessed cheered themselves with hymns such as 'Love Divine, all loves excelling'.

The Church of England, with its usual lethargic response to crisis, failed to meet the needs imposed by the Industrial Revolution. In 1831, while the population of Leeds had soared to over 70,000, the town still had but one parish church. It took the Census of 1851 to wake it up, but by that time England's spiritual thirst was being slaked by poets.

As the blight of industrialism and slum tenements spread, more sensitive souls such as Wordsworth retreated to the dales, to the church that is nature, and the priests which are the elements. Greatly influenced by the writings of Thomas Taylor the Platonist, Wordsworth and Coleridge sought to express the ineffable; Shelley hymned eternal ideas; Blake lived and worked alone with his visionary understanding of that which lies behind the manifest world. Each in his own way was a platonist as defined by Dean Inge, that is, he was aware of the invisible and indivisible without necessarily having studied Plato.

Bunhill Fields, the graveyard of figures such as Blake, Bunyan, Defoe and Susannah Wesley, provides an oasis of peace under the shade of plane trees between City Road and Old Street, London

As the natural beauties of England were ravaged by greed and her freedom-loving people were enslaved by factory employment, the voice of the 'religion of the Spirit' grew loud. It continued to sound in the nineteenth and twentieth centuries, through the words of John Henry Newman and John Ruskin, Tennyson and Gerard Manley Hopkins. It primed a nation for the supreme sacrifice demanded by war, and sustained it through two of them. It manifested itself in the works of charities, particularly those of education and health. The tradition of voluntary work is long-rooted in England. It is only comparatively recently that MPs have been paid to represent their constituencies and the funding of hospitals by voluntary contributions is still within living memory.

Although the English have been moving towards secularism since the Reformation, it was after the two world wars that darkness fell upon English religion. The Church, not recognizing the cause of popular disaffection, struggled in vain to stem the tide of desertion. Various attempts to make itself more attractive, such as, 'modernising' the language of the Bible and the liturgy, appear to have been misguided.

Sociologists now claim that England has become a secular nation, but it may well be that English religiosity remains as it has always been, a stubbornly individual and private affair conducted in seclusion. Lack of attendance at church may not indicate indifference so much as a lack of inspired leadership. When there is enthusiastic leadership, as in the evangelical churches, attendance is huge and, in this age of voluntary attendance, truly phenomenal. It only took a Wesley to have the English bursting into song; it only took a George Fox to plunge them into the

The One remains, the Many
   change and pass;
Heaven's light for ever shines,
   Earth's shadows fly;
Life, like a dome of many-
   coloured glass,
Stains the white radiance
   of Eternity.

PERCY BYSSHE SHELLEY: Adonais

silence of the heart. We are too down-to-earth to be expecting a new Messiah, but we are certainly waiting for a new voice of truth and courage, be it that of preacher or poet.

The history of English religion is so contradictory that it defies any straightforward account. The English who built the finest abbeys in Europe are the English that demolished them. Superb cathedrals were built, only to be vacated for humble chapels. Churches were invested with riches only to be robbed of them. Walls were decorated only to be whitewashed. But whether the English choose to see the Spirit in manifest, architectural glory, or in bare simplicity, there are some constants that unite these apparent irreconcilables. One is the insistence on freedom, freedom to question, ponder and consider, freedom to arrive at one's belief in one's own way and in the light of one's own experience. The other is tolerance. The latter follows the former as surely as the night the day, for if I am to be free to believe what I will, it follows that so must my neighbour be also.

Grasmere, Cumbria, from Loughrigg

The hymns of Charles Wesley can now be heard in High Anglican churches, in Baptist chapels, as well as in Methodist congregations. They are the common property of English Christians, as is the poetry of Bunyan, Milton, Wordsworth and Coleridge. While the organized church, which has never been truly popular, continues to define boundaries between one system of belief and another, the ordinary Englishman, in his more sublime moments, would prefer to see no division between himself and any other being.

The Station whence he look'd was soft and green,
Not giddy yet aerial, with a depth
Of Vale below, a height of hills above.
For rest of body, perfect was the Spot,
All that luxurious nature could desire,
But stirring to the Spirit; who could gaze
And not feel motions there? He thought of clouds
That sail on winds; of Breezes that delight
To play on water, or in endless chase
Pursue each other through the yielding plain
Of grass or corn, over and through and through,
In billow after billow, evermore
Disporting ...
            ... nowhere else is found,
Nowhere (or is it fancy?) can be found
The one sensation that is here; 'tis here,
Here as it found its way into my heart
In childhood, here as it abides by day,
By night, here only; or in chosen minds
That take it with them hence, where'er they go.
Tis, but I cannot name it, tis the sense
Of majesty, and beauty, and repose,
A blended holiness of earth and sky,
Something that makes this individual Spot,
This small Abiding-place of many Men,
A termination and a last retreat,
A Centre, come from whereso'er you will,
A Whole without dependence or defect,
Made for itself; and happy in itself,
Perfect Contentment, Unity entire.

WILLIAM WORDSWORTH:

The Recluse – Home at Grasmere

# Afterword

At the end of the twentieth century we are confronted by change on a scale which has not been previously experienced. In the family, in the workplace, in the nation itself, revolutions are occurring. The history of England shows that we should not fear change; indeed, all that we have now is the product of centuries of reform. But it is gentle reform that succeeds, and not jarring revolution: reform is itself the lifeblood of the fine body of English tradition.

All movements towards world unity are of course to be welcomed, but we should not make the mistake of equating unity with homogeneity. To be one, we do not all have to be the same. Many of the changes which now threaten us are alien. For example, currently it is fashionable to think of 'rights'. Rights are a continental concept. English law has always put the emphasis on duties to preserve freedom, but this freedom will go as the European Courts of Law increase their sway over our judicial system. Similarly 'citizenship' is an alien concept. The British are 'subjects' of the Crown. If this sounds demeaning, consider that *all* Britons are subjects of the Crown, whereas citizenship is usually accompanied by the status of non-citizen. Nations which have citizens also have second-class citizens, called 'migrant workers'. In Britain, anyone who lives here enjoys the same freedom under the law. If we embrace citizenship, the Crown will go, and our society will not be multicultural any more, but will become divided.

It can all begin so simply, with just a thoughtless use of words. Though our body of tradition is fine it is not perfect and many injustices remain to be redressed, but this can only be done harmlessly by reform.

History shows that when one culture meets another, both good and bad may come from it. In our desire for justice, we should guard against grasping at easy solutions from other cultures. The coming years are going to see increasing debate on, amongst other things, the role of monarchy, the form of the House of Lords, and the independence of judges. Such debates will be passionate, but passion should be restrained by reason. If we abandon the golden cord of reason to gain the changes we desire, we risk losing touch with the principles upon which England was founded.

For a definition of reason, we can do no better than to return to that philosopher who has inspired English poets and statesmen so often in the past, Plato. In the *Laws* he describes men and women as the puppets of their affections, pulled this way and that by many strings. These strings are all hard except for the cord of reason, 'called by us the Common Law of the State', which is soft, golden, gentle and beautiful. Through the use of reason, we come to know the difference between right and wrong.

The lack of such powers of discrimination in our society are becoming obvious. To come to know right from wrong, and to discover the principles which underlie our traditions, is the duty upon us all.

Select Bibliography

General

BARKER, Ernest (ed.), *The Character of England*, Oxford 1947

BILLINGS, M., *The English*, London 1991

CHURCHILL, Winston S., *A History of the English-Speaking Peoples*, London 1956

INGE, William Ralph, *England*, London 1953

KEYNES, S. & LAPIDGE, M. (ed.), *Alfred the Great: Asser's 'Life of King Alfred' and Other Contemporary Sources*, London 1983

SCOTT, J. D., *Life in Britain*, London 1956

STENTON, F. M., *Anglo-Saxon England*, Oxford 1971

WHITELOCK, D., *The Beginnings of English Society*, London 1971

The England We See

CAMPBELL, James (ed.), *The Anglo-Saxons*, London 1991

CHAMBERLAIN, Russell, *The English Country Town*, London 1986

CRAWFORD, Peter, *The Living Isles, a Natural History of Britian and Ireland*, London 1985

GIRLING, Richard (ed.), *The Making of the English Garden*, London 1988

HOSKINS, W.G., *The Making of the English Landscape*, London 1971

RACKHAM, Oliver, *The History of the Countryside*, London 1986

RACKHAM, Oliver, *The Last Forest: The Story of Hatfield Forest*, London 1989

WEBSTER, Leslie, and BACKHOUSE, Janet, *The Making of England, Anglo-Saxon Art and Culture*, London 1991

The Law is Above You

BAGEHOT, Walter, *The English Constitution*, London 1929

BLAKE, L. L., *The Young People's Book of Law*, London 1987

BLAKE, L. L., *The Young People's Book of the Constitution*, London 1987

BLAKE, L. L., *Sovereignty*, London 1988

DENNING, Sir Alfred, *Freedom Under the Law*, London 1949

POLLOCK, Sir Frederick, and MAITLAND, F.W., *History of English Law before Edward I*, London 1898/1952

English — the Nation's Treasure

ALEXANDER, Michael (trans.), *The Earliest English Poems*, London 1966

BARFIELD, Owen, *History in English Words*, London 1953

BAUGH, Albert C., *A History of the English Language*, London 1959

BURGESS, Anthony, *A Mouthful of Air*, London 1992

CLAIBORNE, Robert, *The Life and Times of the English Language*, London 1990

JESPERSEN, Otto, *The Growth and Structure of the English Language*, Leipzig 1923

McARTHUR, T., *The Oxford Companion to the English Language*, Oxford 1992

McCRUM, Robert, et al, *The Story of English*, London 1987

QUILLER-COUCH, A., *On the Art of Writing*, Cambridge 1923

QUILLER-COUCH, A., *On the Art of Reading*, Cambridge 1925

WAKELIN, Martyn, *The Archaeology of English*, London 1988

The Open-Air Church

ARMSTRONG, Karen, *The English Mystics of the Fourteenth Century*, London 1991

BEDE, *A History of the English Church and People*, trans. by Leo Sherley-Price, London 1968

BLYTHE, Ronald, *Divine Landscapes*, London 1986

INGE, William Ralph, *The Platonic Tradition in English Religious Thought*, London 1926

GAY, John D., *The Geography of Religion in England*, London 1971

WEBB, J.F. (trans.), *The Age of Bede*, London 1983

INDEX

A

Aachen 119
Acts of Uniformity 65, 134
Addison, Joseph 63, 103
Aidan, St 113
Ailred 123-24
Albinus, abbot 118, 119
Aldeburgh 48
Alfred the Great 7, 19, 33, 34-5,
    52, 53, 67, 72, 79, 80, 87, 88,
    100, 104, 105, 116, 120, 121
Alfred Jewel 120
Alfriston 34
allotments 46
alphabet 100
American English 97
Ancrene Riwle 89, 121
Andrewes, Lancelot 129-30, 134
Angles 18, 60, 112
Anglicanism 127ff
Anglo-Saxon Chronicle 89
Anglo-Saxons 7, 8, 17, 18, 19, 21, 22, 23, 26,
    27, 32, 33, 35, 36, 40, 52, 67, 69, 71, 78,
    80, 82, 84-5, 86, 89, 110, 116, 118, 119
Anselm, St 128
Antony, St 111
Ascham, Sir Roger 126
architecture 114-16
Arthur, king 17
Artorius 17
Asser 33
Athelney 34
Athelstan 67
Auden, W H 48
Augustine, St 61, 111, 113

B

Bacon, Sir Francis 29, 42, 103, 129
Bacon, Friar Roger 73
Bagehot, Walter 66, 68, 69, 70, 72
Bailey, Nathan 97
baptists 133
Bath 33 34 39
Battle of Maldon 86
BBC English 102-3
Beaufort, Lady Margaret 125-26
beauty 7
Becket, Thomas á 124
Becket, Sister Wendy 127
Bede 85, 113, 114, 115, 118, 120, 121
Bedford 133
Beecham, Sir Thomas 78
belgae 17
Beowulf 86
Betjeman, Sir John 48
Bewcastle Cross 111
Bible, authorized version 96, 105, 108, 129ff
Bible, translations of 96, 105
Bill of Rights 64, 66

Binchester 27
Black Death 122
Blackstone, Sir William 54, 58
Blake, William 10, 48, 108, 135, 136, 137
Blue, Rabbi Lionel 115
Boethius 8, 88, 91, 92, 120, 128
Boswell, James 98
Bracton, Henry 59, 60
bridges 36
Bristol 62
Britten, Benjamin 48
Brown, Capability 25, 31, 46
brythons 17
Buckinghamshire 38
Bunhill Fields 137
Bunyan, John 10, 108, 133, 137, 139
Burford 29
Burgess, Anthony 102
Burghal Hideage 34
burhs 34
Burke, Edmund 52, 65, 68, 127
Burnham Beeches 23
Buxton 39
Byrd, William 48, 129

C

Cabinet, the 70
Caedmon 85-6, 117
Cambridge Platonists 128, 135
Cambridge University 72ff, 125-6, 131
canals 37
Canterbury 33, 111
Caroline Divines 134
Carolingian renaissance 119
Cassian, St John 8, 111
Celts 17, 18, 26, 33
Charlemagne 67, 119
Charles II, king 14, 128
Charles, Prince of Wales 42-3, 62
Chaucer, Geoffrey 79, 82, 91,
    92, 94, 100, 121, 122
Cheke, Sir John 126
Chelsea Flower Show 46
Chelsea Physick Garden 42
Cheltenham 39
Chester-le-Street 115
Chesterton, G K 7
Chichester 34
Chilterns 133
Christianity 32, 34, 41, 52, 53, 60,
    85, 86, 108ff
Chrysostom, St John 8
Church, the 54, 85, 108ff
churches 28
church spires 28
Churchill, Sir Winston 18, 54, 59, 72, 84,
    88, 89, 91 104, 105
Cistercian order 124
civil service 70
Clare, John 31

Clifford, Lady Anne 24
Cloud of Unknowing 113, 121, 122, 123
Coke, Sir Edward 50, 60, 61
Coleridge, Samuel Taylor 48, 108,
    128, 136, 139
Colet, John 125-26
Colman, Abbot 116
Columba, St 111
Common Law 31, 52, 63, 64, 65, 69
Constable, John 48, 135
constitution 65, 66, 69, 74
Constitutions of Clarendon 61
copyholder 61-2
Cornwall 15, 18
coronation 67
Corpus Christi College, Oxford 126
Cotman, John Sell 48
Cotton, Sir Robert 86
Cotswolds 14, 28
Coverdale, Miles 96, 130
Cranmer, Sir Thomas 130
Cricklade 34
Crome, John 48
Cromwell, Oliver 134
crusades 34
custom 53, 54, 103
Cuthbert, St 113-16, 121

D

Danelaw, the 34
Danes, the 19
Daniel, bishop 119
Danvers, John 42
dark ages 54, 60
Davies, Sir John 56
Defoe, Daniel 137
Delius 48
Denning, Lord Alfred 52, 53, 56, 60, 64, 65
Devlin, Sir Patrick 57
Devon 15
Dickens, Charles 100
dictionaries 97-100, 103
Disraeli, Benjamin 72
Ditchley Park 89
Donne, John 42, 48, 74, 129, 130
dooms 52, 55
Drake, Sir Francis 18
Dunstable 48
Dunstan, St 67
Durham cathedral 114-16, 117

E

East Anglia 15, 33, 48
Economist, The 66
Edward the Confessor 67, 116
Edward I, king 36
Edward IV, king 60
Elgar, Edward 47, 48
Eliot, T S 48, 96, 128

Elizabeth I, queen 126, 129
Elizabeth II, queen 65, 66, 67, 69
Emmanuel College, Cambridge 128
enclosures 27, 30, 31
Erasmus 64, 125-26
Escombe chapel 27, 118
Esius, abbot 119
Essex 33, 38
European Union 104
Evelyn, John 26
Exeter 73

F

factories 36
Farne islands 113
Ferrar, Nicholas 131
Ficino, Marsilio 92, 125, 128
Fisher, St John 126
Flixborough 117
forest 23, 25
forest laws 25
Fortescue, Sir John 60, 63
Fountains abbey 125
Fowler, H W 81
Fox, George 106, 134, 138
Frederick, Prince of Wales 41
freedom 7, 22, 74, 80, 81, 88, 95
Fry, Christopher 84
Fuller, Thomas 60

G

gardens 40ff
Garrick, David 103
Gawain and the Green Knight 90
George, St 116
George V, king 68
George VI, king 68
Girtin, Thomas 48
Gladstone, Sir William 66, 72
Glanville, Ranulf 57
Glorious Revolution 64
Gloucester 33
Gloucestershire 48
goidels 17
Goldsworthy, Andy 114
Graves, Robert 87
Gray, Thomas 83
Gray's Inn 63
Gregory the Great, pope 60, 61, 88, 111, 121
Grosseteste, Robert, bishop 90
Grocyn, William 125
Guthram 34, 87

H

Hadrian's wall 55
Hampshire 18
Hampton Court 40
Hawksmoor, Nicholas 58
hedges 30-1
Henry II, king 56, 57, 58, 124
Henry III, king 59, 90
Henry V, king 90
Henry VII, king 125
Henry VIII, king 126
Heptonstall 136
herbaceous borders 46, 47
Herbert, George 42, 48, 128-29, 131-32, 135

Herbert, Magdalena 129
Herefordshire 28, 48
Hertfordshire 38
Hexam 123
hideage system 22, 34
Highgrove House 42-3
Hild, abbess 117
Hilton, Walter 123
Hobbes, Thomas 64, 128
Holdsworth, Sir William 60
Holinshed's *Chronicle* 126
Holst, Gustav 48
Hood, Robin 25
Hooker, Sir Joseph 42
Hooker, Richard 53, 64, 103, 126-28
Hopkins, Gerard Manley 26, 108, 118, 137
horticulture 40ff
Hoskins, W G 21
Howard, Henry, Earl of Surrey 95

I

Industrial Revolution 36ff, 135, 136
industry 37
Inge, William 108, 125, 128, 137
Inner Temple 63
Inns of Court 61, 63
International Phonetic Alphabet 102
Iona 111, 112

J

James I, king 60, 126, 129
James II, king 64
jargon 105
Jarrow 117, 118
Jeffries, Richard 19
Jekyll, Gertrude 47
Jespersen, Otto 81
John of Gaunt 122
John of Salisbury 57
John I, king 25, 58
Johnson, Samuel 97, 98, 103
Jones, Sir William 55
Jonson, Ben 76
Julian of Norwich 117, 123
jury system 57ff
justice 7, 22, 52, 64, 74, 123
Justinian, emperor 54

K

Keats, John 48
Kent 33, 39
Kent, William 25, 31, 42, 47
Kew gardens 42, 44
Kilvert, Rev. Francis 25

L

land tenure 21
Lanfranc 55, 56
Langland, William 10, 48, 122, 123, 124
Langton, Stephen 59
language 7, 78ff, 121, 131-33
Lao Tsu 110
latitudinarians 135
law 7, 50ff
Law, William 135
Lawrence of Ludlow 34

Laxton 32
Leamington Spa 39
Lee, Laurie 21
Leeds 38, 136
Leighton Bromswold 56
Levens Hall 44
Lichfield 103
Linacre, Thomas 125
Lincoln 51, 73, 115
Lincoln's Inn 63
Lindisfarne 112, 115, 116, 118, 120
Lindisfarne Gospels 78, 119
Little Gidding 131
Little Rollright 28
Liverpool 38
London 33, 38-9
London, Corporation of 23
Lorca, Federico Garcia 8

M

Macauley, Thomas Babington 72
MacLaren, Andrew 80
Macmillan, Lord Hugh Pattison, 64
Magna Carta 25, 59, 66
Maitland, Frederick William 63
Mansfield, Lord William Murray 62
Marvell, Andrew 48
Mary Tudor, queen 126
Manchester 38
masonry, art of 27
measure 82
Mendelssohn, Felix 23
Mercia 33
Merton, Walter de 73
Methodists 133, 135-36
Middle Temple 63
Middlesborough 37, 135
Middlesex 38
Midlands 15
Milton, John 95, 108, 132-33, 139
Moccas Park 24
monarchy 66, 68-9
monasticism 111
Montfort, Simon de 36, 90
More, Sir Thomas 29, 63, 125-26
More, Henry 128, 135
Morris, William 36
Morwenstow 49
music and musicians 48, 132
mystics 123, 135

N

National Council for the Conservation
  of Plants and Gardens 44
neoplatonism 91, 125
Nerthus, goddess 110
Newman, John Henry 137
nonconformism 133 ff
Normans 10, 23, 25, 28, 36, 83, 89,
  114, 115, 121, 124
Northamptonshire 28
Northumberland 33
Northumbria, Golden Age of 119
Norwich School 48
Nothelm 119
Nottingham 38
Nuneham Courtenay 17

O

oak trees 26, 80
Old Bailey 64
Oswald, St 111, 112
O'Sullivan, Richard 60, 62, 63
Oxford 32
Oxford Botanic Garden 42
Oxford English Dictionary 98-9
Oxford University 10, 17, 58, 72ff, 125, 135

P

pagans 110, 124
Painswick 29
painters 48
parks 25
Parliament 29, 30, 31, 36, 46, 64, 69, 70-2
Parry, Hubert 48
Patrick, St 111
peace 7
Peasants' Revolt 122, 124
Pendle Hill 134
Pepys, Samuel 18
Petition of Right 66
Pickles, James 105
Pitt, William 72
Plato 8, 92, 108, 128
platonism 8, 9, 57, 91, 108, 120, 126-28, 137
poets and poetry 10, 48, 81, 82, 85, 86, 95, 105, 108, 132, 136-39
Powicke, Sir Maurice 73
presbyterianism 134
prime minister 70
pronunciation 101-3
Purcell, Henry 48, 132

Q

Quakers 133-34
Quiller-Couch, Sir Arthur 15, 96, 104

R

Rackham, Oliver 26
Raleigh, Sir Walter 18, 103
Ramblers Association 40
Rees-Mogg, William 109
Reform Act 70
Reformation 127, 128, 135, 137
Renaissance 41, 42, 57, 71, 86, 88, 90, 92, 105, 113, 119-20, 124, 126-28, 131
Restoration 133, 134
rhythm 71, 81, 82, 85, 88, 96, 117, 131
Richard I, king 35
Richard II, king 122
Richardson, Charles 98
Rievaulx Abbey 123-24
rivers 37
Rolle, Richard 117, 123
Roman Catholicism 108
Roman Church 10, 109
Romano-Britons 18
Romans 17, 18, 27, 32-3, 41, 53, 54
Romney 27
Rosebery, Archibald Philip Primrose, 5th Earl of, 72
Royal Botanic Gardens 42
Royal Horticulture Society 44, 46

royalty 66
Rule of St. Benedict 67, 111, 123
runes 100
Runnymede 59
Ruskin, John 16, 81, 132, 137

S

St German, Christopher 61, 63
St Paul's Grammar School 125, 133
Salisbury 73
Scotus, Duns 128
seafaring 18
Shakespeare, William 29, 48, 67, 79, 85, 90, 93, 94, 95, 103, 105, 121, 127, 131
Shaw, George Bernard 67, 102
sheep 28-9
Sheffield 38
Shelley, Percy Bysshe 136, 137
Sherwood Forest 25
Shropshire 28, 35, 48
Sidney, Sir Philip 103, 125
Skipton 37
Skipton Castle 25
Slad 20-1
slavery 61-2, 136
slums 37
Smith, John 128
Smith, Sidney 97
Society of Friends 134
Socrates 110
Somerset 34
sonnets 85, 132
sovereignty 69
speech 71, 85
spelling 97, 101
Spenser, Edmund 103
steam power 37
stewardship 26
Stillingfleet, Edward 135
Stoke Poges 83
Stokesay Castle 35
Surrey 38
Sussex 33, 34
Synod of Whitby 85, 87, 116, 118
Swinbrook 13

T

Tallis, Thomas 48, 132
Taverner, John 48, 132
Taylor, Jeremy 134
Taylor, Thomas 136
Tennyson, Lord Alfred 108, 137
Theodore of Tarsus 111
Thomas, Edward 12, 22, 40, 48
Tillotson, John 135
tolerance 7, 127, 138
towns 32ff
Tradescant, John 41
Trafalgar, battle of 18
trees 26, 80
truth 7, 74, 76, 80, 95, 105
Tunbridge Wells 39
Turner, JWM 48
Tyndale, William 96, 130

U

Uffington 34, 107
university 63, 72ff

V

Vaughan Williams, Ralph 48
Victoria, queen 68
Vikings 19, 33, 34, 83, 84, 86, 87, 89, 115, 119, 120
villages 21, 22
village shows 46
villein 23, 61

W

Wales 18
Wallingford 34
Walton, Isaak 66
Wareham 34
Warwickshire 103
watermills 36
Wearmouth 117, 118
weather 15
Wells Cathedral 132
Wells-next-the-Sea 15
Wesley, Charles 139
Wesley, John 135-36, 138
Wesley, Susannah 137
Wessex 33, 34
Westminster 67, 68-9, 71
Westmoreland 18
West Stow 18
Whichcote, Benjamin 128
Whitby 85, 87
Wilberforce, William 61, 62
Wildy and Sons, bookshop 61
William of Orange 42, 64
William the Conqueror 23, 25, 55
Winchester 34, 67
Windrush Valley 13
Windsor 57, 59, 69
wisdom 80, 88, 108
Wisley 44
Woden 66, 110
wool trade 28-9, 35
Wordsworth, William 10, 15, 36, 37, 48, 49, 95, 108, 136, 139
Wycliffe 122, 123, 125, 130

Y

yeoman farmers 30-1, 36, 62
York 33, 115, 118
Yorkshire 15

Z

Zoroastra 110